ISBN 0-8373-3928-6

C-3928 CAREER EXAMINATION SERIES

This is your PASSBOOK® for...

Emergency Management Services Specialist

Test Preparation Study Guide

Questions & Answers

EAST NORTHPORT PUBLIC LIBRARY
EAST NORTHPORT, NEW YORK

NLC

NATIONAL LEARNING CORPORATION

Copyright © 2014 by

National Learning Corporation

212 Michael Drive, Syosset, New York 11791

All rights reserved, including the right of reproduction in whole or in part, in any form or by any means, electronic or mechanical, including photocopying, recording, or by any information storage and retrieval system, without permission in writing from the Publisher.

(516) 921-8888
(800) 645-6337
FAX: (516) 921-8743
www.passbooks.com
sales @ passbooks.com
info @ passbooks.com

PRINTED IN THE UNITED STATES OF AMERICA

PASSBOOK®
NOTICE

This book is SOLELY intended for, is sold ONLY to, and its use is RESTRICTED to *individual*, bona fide applicants or candidates who qualify by virtue of having seriously filed applications for appropriate license, certificate, professional and/or promotional advancement, higher school matriculation, scholarship, or other legitimate requirements of educational and/or governmental authorities.

This book is NOT intended for use, class instruction, tutoring, training, duplication, copying, reprinting, excerption, or adaptation, etc., by:

(1) Other publishers

(2) Proprietors and/or Instructors of "Coaching" and/or Preparatory Courses

(3) Personnel and/or Training Divisions of commercial, industrial, and governmental organizations

(4) Schools, colleges, or universities and/or their departments and staffs, including teachers and other personnel

(5) Testing Agencies or Bureaus

(6) Study groups which seek by the purchase of a single volume to copy and/or duplicate and/or adapt this material for use by the group as a whole without having purchased individual volumes for each of the members of the group

(7) Et al.

Such persons would be in violation of appropriate Federal and State statutes.

PROVISION OF LICENSING AGREEMENTS. — Recognized educational commercial, industrial, and governmental institutions and organizations, and others legitimately engaged in educational pursuits, including training, testing, and measurement activities, may address a request for a licensing agreement to the copyright owners, who will determine whether, and under what conditions, including fees and charges, the materials in this book may be used by them. In other words, a licensing facility exists for the legitimate use of the material in this book on other than an individual basis. However, it is asseverated and affirmed here that the material in this book *CANNOT* be used without the receipt of the express permission of such a licensing agreement from the Publishers.

NATIONAL LEARNING CORPORATION
212 Michael Drive
Syosset, New York 11791

Inquiries re licensing agreements should be addressed to:
The President
National Learning Corporation
212 Michael Drive
Syosset, New York 11791

PASSBOOK SERIES®

THE *PASSBOOK SERIES®* has been created to prepare applicants and candidates for the ultimate academic battlefield – the examination room.

At some time in our lives, each and every one of us may be required to take an examination – for validation, matriculation, admission, qualification, registration, certification, or licensure.

Based on the assumption that every applicant or candidate has met the basic formal educational standards, has taken the required number of courses, and read the necessary texts, the *PASSBOOK SERIES®* furnishes the one special preparation which may assure passing with confidence, instead of failing with insecurity. Examination questions – together with answers – are furnished as the basic vehicle for study so that the mysteries of the examination and its compounding difficulties may be eliminated or diminished by a sure method.

This book is meant to help you pass your examination provided that you qualify and are serious in your objective.

The entire field is reviewed through the huge store of content information which is succinctly presented through a provocative and challenging approach – the question-and-answer method.

A climate of success is established by furnishing the correct answers at the end of each test.

You soon learn to recognize types of questions, forms of questions, and patterns of questioning. You may even begin to anticipate expected outcomes.

You perceive that many questions are repeated or adapted so that you can gain acute insights, which may enable you to score many sure points.

You learn how to confront new questions, or types of questions, and to attack them confidently and work out the correct answers.

You note objectives and emphases, and recognize pitfalls and dangers, so that you may make positive educational adjustments.

Moreover, you are kept fully informed in relation to new concepts, methods, practices, and directions in the field.

You discover that you are actually taking the examination all the time: you are preparing for the examination by "taking" an examination, not by reading extraneous and/or supererogatory textbooks.

In short, this PASSBOOK®, used directedly, should be an important factor in helping you to pass your test.

EMERGENCY MANAGEMENT SERVICES SPECIALIST

DUTIES:

Assists in planning and coordinating programs by which the County may properly carry out its emergency preparedness and fire safety responsibilities;

Assists in planning and coordinating meetings of various committees and advisory boards involved in the operations of the County Fire & Emergency Management Services Department;

Assists with the procurement and inventory of facilities, equipment, and services required for the carrying out of a comprehensive fire and emergency preparedness program;

Meets with local officials to review special problems, procedures and directives, and the coordination of local fire and emergency programs;

Assists with administrative duties and implementation of federal contribution programs and other fiscal aid programs;

Performs specific tasks related to intra-county and inter-county emergency management operations and mutual aid functions;

Assists with plans for use of emergency communications systems;

May act as liaison between the County and other governmental agencies involved in the coordination of Emergency Management Service operations;

Assists in recruiting volunteers to assist with programs and Emergency Services functions from among public officials, employees, and the general public;

Assists in promoting the activities of the Emergency Services Department through public speeches, the distribution of literature, use of the media for public information, education, and training;

Assists in preparing grant requests and coordinating the filing of reimbursement claims by various municipalities in the County to State and Federal agencies;

Assists in planning and coordinating the efforts of County agencies during natural or man-made emergencies;

Acts for and in place of the Director of Fire and Emergency Management in their absence;

Prepares a variety of records and reports.

SCOPE OF EXAMINATION: Written test will cover knowledge, skills, and/or abilities in such areas as:

1. Communicating and interacting with the public
2. Fire prevention, fire inspections, and fire hazards
3. The mutual aid and emergency preparedness process
4. Preparing written material
5. Principles and practices of staff development and training
6. Supervision
7. Understanding and interpreting fire codes

HOW TO TAKE A TEST

I. YOU MUST PASS AN EXAMINATION

A. *WHAT EVERY CANDIDATE SHOULD KNOW*

Examination applicants often ask us for help in preparing for the written test. What can I study in advance? What kinds of questions will be asked? How will the test be given? How will the papers be graded?

As an applicant for a civil service examination, you may be wondering about some of these things. Our purpose here is to suggest effective methods of advance study and to describe civil service examinations.

Your chances for success on this examination can be increased if you know how to prepare. Those "pre-examination jitters" can be reduced if you know what to expect. You can even experience an adventure in good citizenship if you know why civil service exams are given.

B. *WHY ARE CIVIL SERVICE EXAMINATIONS GIVEN?*

Civil service examinations are important to you in two ways. As a citizen, you want public jobs filled by employees who know how to do their work. As a job seeker, you want a fair chance to compete for that job on an equal footing with other candidates. The best-known means of accomplishing this two-fold goal is the competitive examination.

Exams are widely publicized throughout the nation. They may be administered for jobs in federal, state, city, municipal, town or village governments or agencies.

Any citizen may apply, with some limitations, such as the age or residence of applicants. Your experience and education may be reviewed to see whether you meet the requirements for the particular examination. When these requirements exist, they are reasonable and applied consistently to all applicants. Thus, a competitive examination may cause you some uneasiness now, but it is your privilege and safeguard.

C. *HOW ARE CIVIL SERVICE EXAMS DEVELOPED?*

Examinations are carefully written by trained technicians who are specialists in the field known as "psychological measurement," in consultation with recognized authorities in the field of work that the test will cover. These experts recommend the subject matter areas or skills to be tested; only those knowledges or skills important to your success on the job are included. The most reliable books and source materials available are used as references. Together, the experts and technicians judge the difficulty level of the questions.

Test technicians know how to phrase questions so that the problem is clearly stated. Their ethics do not permit "trick" or "catch" questions. Questions may have been tried out on sample groups, or subjected to statistical analysis, to determine their usefulness.

Written tests are often used in combination with performance tests, ratings of training and experience, and oral interviews. All of these measures combine to form the best-known means of finding the right person for the right job.

II. HOW TO PASS THE WRITTEN TEST

A. NATURE OF THE EXAMINATION

To prepare intelligently for civil service examinations, you should know how they differ from school examinations you have taken. In school you were assigned certain definite pages to read or subjects to cover. The examination questions were quite detailed and usually emphasized memory. Civil service exams, on the other hand, try to discover your present ability to perform the duties of a position, plus your potentiality to learn these duties. In other words, a civil service exam attempts to predict how successful you will be. Questions cover such a broad area that they cannot be as minute and detailed as school exam questions.

In the public service similar kinds of work, or positions, are grouped together in one "class." This process is known as *position-classification*. All the positions in a class are paid according to the salary range for that class. One class title covers all of these positions, and they are all tested by the same examination.

B. FOUR BASIC STEPS

1) Study the announcement

How, then, can you know what subjects to study? Our best answer is: "Learn as much as possible about the class of positions for which you've applied." The exam will test the knowledge, skills and abilities needed to do the work.

Your most valuable source of information about the position you want is the official exam announcement. This announcement lists the training and experience qualifications. Check these standards and apply only if you come reasonably close to meeting them.

The brief description of the position in the examination announcement offers some clues to the subjects which will be tested. Think about the job itself. Review the duties in your mind. Can you perform them, or are there some in which you are rusty? Fill in the blank spots in your preparation.

Many jurisdictions preview the written test in the exam announcement by including a section called "Knowledge and Abilities Required," "Scope of the Examination," or some similar heading. Here you will find out specifically what fields will be tested.

2) Review your own background

Once you learn in general what the position is all about, and what you need to know to do the work, ask yourself which subjects you already know fairly well and which need improvement. You may wonder whether to concentrate on improving your strong areas or on building some background in your fields of weakness. When the announcement has specified "some knowledge" or "considerable knowledge," or has used adjectives like "beginning principles of…" or "advanced … methods," you can get a clue as to the number and difficulty of questions to be asked in any given field. More questions, and hence broader coverage, would be included for those subjects which are more important in the work. Now weigh your strengths and weaknesses against the job requirements and prepare accordingly.

3) Determine the level of the position

Another way to tell how intensively you should prepare is to understand the level of the job for which you are applying. Is it the entering level? In other words, is this the position in which beginners in a field of work are hired? Or is it an intermediate or advanced level? Sometimes this is indicated by such words as "Junior" or "Senior" in the class title. Other jurisdictions use Roman numerals to designate the level – Clerk I, Clerk II, for example. The word "Supervisor" sometimes appears in the title. If the level is not indicated by the title, check the description of duties. Will you be working under very close supervision, or will you have responsibility for independent decisions in this work?

4) Choose appropriate study materials

Now that you know the subjects to be examined and the relative amount of each subject to be covered, you can choose suitable study materials. For beginning level jobs, or even advanced ones, if you have a pronounced weakness in some aspect of your training, read a modern, standard textbook in that field. Be sure it is up to date and has general coverage. Such books are normally available at your library, and the librarian will be glad to help you locate one. For entry-level positions, questions of appropriate difficulty are chosen – neither highly advanced questions, nor those too simple. Such questions require careful thought but not advanced training.

If the position for which you are applying is technical or advanced, you will read more advanced, specialized material. If you are already familiar with the basic principles of your field, elementary textbooks would waste your time. Concentrate on advanced textbooks and technical periodicals. Think through the concepts and review difficult problems in your field.

These are all general sources. You can get more ideas on your own initiative, following these leads. For example, training manuals and publications of the government agency which employs workers in your field can be useful, particularly for technical and professional positions. A letter or visit to the government department involved may result in more specific study suggestions, and certainly will provide you with a more definite idea of the exact nature of the position you are seeking.

III. KINDS OF TESTS

Tests are used for purposes other than measuring knowledge and ability to perform specified duties. For some positions, it is equally important to test ability to make adjustments to new situations or to profit from training. In others, basic mental abilities not dependent on information are essential. Questions which test these things may not appear as pertinent to the duties of the position as those which test for knowledge and information. Yet they are often highly important parts of a fair examination. For very general questions, it is almost impossible to help you direct your study efforts. What we can do is to point out some of the more common of these general abilities needed in public service positions and describe some typical questions.

1) General information

Broad, general information has been found useful for predicting job success in some kinds of work. This is tested in a variety of ways, from vocabulary lists to questions about current events. Basic background in some field of work, such as sociology or economics, may be sampled in a group of questions. Often these are principles which have become familiar to most persons through exposure rather than through formal training. It is difficult to advise you how to study for these questions; being alert to the world around you is our best suggestion.

2) Verbal ability

An example of an ability needed in many positions is verbal or language ability. Verbal ability is, in brief, the ability to use and understand words. Vocabulary and grammar tests are typical measures of this ability. Reading comprehension or paragraph interpretation questions are common in many kinds of civil service tests. You are given a paragraph of written material and asked to find its central meaning.

3) Numerical ability

Number skills can be tested by the familiar arithmetic problem, by checking paired lists of numbers to see which are alike and which are different, or by interpreting charts and graphs. In the latter test, a graph may be printed in the test booklet which you are asked to use as the basis for answering questions.

4) Observation

A popular test for law-enforcement positions is the observation test. A picture is shown to you for several minutes, then taken away. Questions about the picture test your ability to observe both details and larger elements.

5) Following directions

In many positions in the public service, the employee must be able to carry out written instructions dependably and accurately. You may be given a chart with several columns, each column listing a variety of information. The questions require you to carry out directions involving the information given in the chart.

6) Skills and aptitudes

Performance tests effectively measure some manual skills and aptitudes. When the skill is one in which you are trained, such as typing or shorthand, you can practice. These tests are often very much like those given in business school or high school courses. For many of the other skills and aptitudes, however, no short-time preparation can be made. Skills and abilities natural to you or that you have developed throughout your lifetime are being tested.

Many of the general questions just described provide all the data needed to answer the questions and ask you to use your reasoning ability to find the answers. Your best preparation for these tests, as well as for tests of facts and ideas, is to be at your physical and mental best. You, no doubt, have your own methods of getting into an exam-taking mood and keeping "in shape." The next section lists some ideas on this subject.

IV. KINDS OF QUESTIONS

Only rarely is the "essay" question, which you answer in narrative form, used in civil service tests. Civil service tests are usually of the short-answer type. Full instructions for answering these questions will be given to you at the examination. But in case this is your first experience with short-answer questions and separate answer sheets, here is what you need to know:

1) Multiple-choice Questions

Most popular of the short-answer questions is the "multiple choice" or "best answer" question. It can be used, for example, to test for factual knowledge, ability to solve problems or judgment in meeting situations found at work.

A multiple-choice question is normally one of three types—
- It can begin with an incomplete statement followed by several possible endings. You are to find the one ending which *best* completes the statement, although some of the others may not be entirely wrong.
- It can also be a complete statement in the form of a question which is answered by choosing one of the statements listed.
- It can be in the form of a problem – again you select the best answer.

Here is an example of a multiple-choice question with a discussion which should give you some clues as to the method for choosing the right answer:

When an employee has a complaint about his assignment, the action which will *best* help him overcome his difficulty is to
 A. discuss his difficulty with his coworkers
 B. take the problem to the head of the organization
 C. take the problem to the person who gave him the assignment
 D. say nothing to anyone about his complaint

In answering this question, you should study each of the choices to find which is best. Consider choice "A" – Certainly an employee may discuss his complaint with fellow employees, but no change or improvement can result, and the complaint remains unresolved. Choice "B" is a poor choice since the head of the organization probably does not know what assignment you have been given, and taking your problem to him is known as "going over the head" of the supervisor. The supervisor, or person who made the assignment, is the person who can clarify it or correct any injustice. Choice "C" is, therefore, correct. To say nothing, as in choice "D," is unwise. Supervisors have and interest in knowing the problems employees are facing, and the employee is seeking a solution to his problem.

2) True/False Questions

The "true/false" or "right/wrong" form of question is sometimes used. Here a complete statement is given. Your job is to decide whether the statement is right or wrong.

SAMPLE: A person-to-person long-distance telephone call costs less than a station-to-station call to the same city.

This statement is wrong, or false, since person-to-person calls are more expensive.

This is not a complete list of all possible question forms, although most of the others are variations of these common types. You will always get complete directions for answering questions. Be sure you understand *how* to mark your answers – ask questions until you do.

V. RECORDING YOUR ANSWERS

For an examination with very few applicants, you may be told to record your answers in the test booklet itself. Separate answer sheets are much more common. If this separate answer sheet is to be scored by machine – and this is often the case – it is highly important that you mark your answers correctly in order to get credit.

An electric scoring machine is often used in civil service offices because of the speed with which papers can be scored. Machine-scored answer sheets must be marked with a pencil, which will be given to you. This pencil has a high graphite content which responds to the electric scoring machine. As a matter of fact, stray dots may register as answers, so do not let your pencil rest on the answer sheet while you are pondering the correct answer. Also, if your pencil lead breaks or is otherwise defective, ask for another.

Since the answer sheet will be dropped in a slot in the scoring machine, be careful not to bend the corners or get the paper crumpled.

The answer sheet normally has five vertical columns of numbers, with 30 numbers to a column. These numbers correspond to the question numbers in your test booklet. After each number, going across the page are four or five pairs of dotted lines. These short dotted lines have small letters or numbers above them. The first two pairs may also have a "T" or "F" above the letters. This indicates that the first two pairs only are to be used if the questions are of the true-false type. If the questions are multiple choice, disregard the "T" and "F" and pay attention only to the small letters or numbers.

Answer your questions in the manner of the sample that follows:

32. The largest city in the United States is
    A. Washington, D.C.
    B. New York City
    C. Chicago
    D. Detroit
    E. San Francisco

1) Choose the answer you think is best. (New York City is the largest, so "B" is correct.)
2) Find the row of dotted lines numbered the same as the question you are answering. (Find row number 32)
3) Find the pair of dotted lines corresponding to the answer. (Find the pair of lines under the mark "B.")
4) Make a solid black mark between the dotted lines.

VI. BEFORE THE TEST

Common sense will help you find procedures to follow to get ready for an examination. Too many of us, however, overlook these sensible measures. Indeed, nervousness and fatigue have been found to be the most serious reasons why applicants fail to do their best on civil service tests. Here is a list of reminders:

- Begin your preparation early – Don't wait until the last minute to go scurrying around for books and materials or to find out what the position is all about.
- Prepare continuously – An hour a night for a week is better than an all-night cram session. This has been definitely established. What is more, a night a

week for a month will return better dividends than crowding your study into a shorter period of time.
- Locate the place of the exam – You have been sent a notice telling you when and where to report for the examination. If the location is in a different town or otherwise unfamiliar to you, it would be well to inquire the best route and learn something about the building.
- Relax the night before the test – Allow your mind to rest. Do not study at all that night. Plan some mild recreation or diversion; then go to bed early and get a good night's sleep.
- Get up early enough to make a leisurely trip to the place for the test – This way unforeseen events, traffic snarls, unfamiliar buildings, etc. will not upset you.
- Dress comfortably – A written test is not a fashion show. You will be known by number and not by name, so wear something comfortable.
- Leave excess paraphernalia at home – Shopping bags and odd bundles will get in your way. You need bring only the items mentioned in the official notice you received; usually everything you need is provided. Do not bring reference books to the exam. They will only confuse those last minutes and be taken away from you when in the test room.
- Arrive somewhat ahead of time – If because of transportation schedules you must get there very early, bring a newspaper or magazine to take your mind off yourself while waiting.
- Locate the examination room – When you have found the proper room, you will be directed to the seat or part of the room where you will sit. Sometimes you are given a sheet of instructions to read while you are waiting. Do not fill out any forms until you are told to do so; just read them and be prepared.
- Relax and prepare to listen to the instructions
- If you have any physical problem that may keep you from doing your best, be sure to tell the test administrator. If you are sick or in poor health, you really cannot do your best on the exam. You can come back and take the test some other time.

VII. AT THE TEST

The day of the test is here and you have the test booklet in your hand. The temptation to get going is very strong. Caution! There is more to success than knowing the right answers. You must know how to identify your papers and understand variations in the type of short-answer question used in this particular examination. Follow these suggestions for maximum results from your efforts:

1) Cooperate with the monitor

The test administrator has a duty to create a situation in which you can be as much at ease as possible. He will give instructions, tell you when to begin, check to see that you are marking your answer sheet correctly, and so on. He is not there to guard you, although he will see that your competitors do not take unfair advantage. He wants to help you do your best.

2) Listen to all instructions

Don't jump the gun! Wait until you understand all directions. In most civil service tests you get more time than you need to answer the questions. So don't be in a hurry.

Read each word of instructions until you clearly understand the meaning. Study the examples, listen to all announcements and follow directions. Ask questions if you do not understand what to do.

3) Identify your papers

Civil service exams are usually identified by number only. You will be assigned a number; you must not put your name on your test papers. Be sure to copy your number correctly. Since more than one exam may be given, copy your exact examination title.

4) Plan your time

Unless you are told that a test is a "speed" or "rate of work" test, speed itself is usually not important. Time enough to answer all the questions will be provided, but this does not mean that you have all day. An overall time limit has been set. Divide the total time (in minutes) by the number of questions to determine the approximate time you have for each question.

5) Do not linger over difficult questions

If you come across a difficult question, mark it with a paper clip (useful to have along) and come back to it when you have been through the booklet. One caution if you do this – be sure to skip a number on your answer sheet as well. Check often to be sure that you have not lost your place and that you are marking in the row numbered the same as the question you are answering.

6) Read the questions

Be sure you know what the question asks! Many capable people are unsuccessful because they failed to *read* the questions correctly.

7) Answer all questions

Unless you have been instructed that a penalty will be deducted for incorrect answers, it is better to guess than to omit a question.

8) Speed tests

It is often better NOT to guess on speed tests. It has been found that on timed tests people are tempted to spend the last few seconds before time is called in marking answers at random – without even reading them – in the hope of picking up a few extra points. To discourage this practice, the instructions may warn you that your score will be "corrected" for guessing. That is, a penalty will be applied. The incorrect answers will be deducted from the correct ones, or some other penalty formula will be used.

9) Review your answers

If you finish before time is called, go back to the questions you guessed or omitted to give them further thought. Review other answers if you have time.

10) Return your test materials

If you are ready to leave before others have finished or time is called, take ALL your materials to the monitor and leave quietly. Never take any test material with you. The monitor can discover whose papers are not complete, and taking a test booklet may be grounds for disqualification.

VIII. EXAMINATION TECHNIQUES

1) Read the general instructions carefully. These are usually printed on the first page of the exam booklet. As a rule, these instructions refer to the timing of the examination; the fact that you should not start work until the signal and must stop work at a signal, etc. If there are any *special* instructions, such as a choice of questions to be answered, make sure that you note this instruction carefully.

2) When you are ready to start work on the examination, that is as soon as the signal has been given, read the instructions to each question booklet, underline any key words or phrases, such as *least, best, outline, describe* and the like. In this way you will tend to answer as requested rather than discover on reviewing your paper that you *listed without describing*, that you selected the *worst* choice rather than the *best* choice, etc.

3) If the examination is of the objective or multiple-choice type – that is, each question will also give a series of possible answers: A, B, C or D, and you are called upon to select the best answer and write the letter next to that answer on your answer paper – it is advisable to start answering each question in turn. There may be anywhere from 50 to 100 such questions in the three or four hours allotted and you can see how much time would be taken if you read through all the questions before beginning to answer any. Furthermore, if you come across a question or group of questions which you know would be difficult to answer, it would undoubtedly affect your handling of all the other questions.

4) If the examination is of the essay type and contains but a few questions, it is a moot point as to whether you should read all the questions before starting to answer any one. Of course, if you are given a choice – say five out of seven and the like – then it is essential to read all the questions so you can eliminate the two that are most difficult. If, however, you are asked to answer all the questions, there may be danger in trying to answer the easiest one first because you may find that you will spend too much time on it. The best technique is to answer the first question, then proceed to the second, etc.

5) Time your answers. Before the exam begins, write down the time it started, then add the time allowed for the examination and write down the time it must be completed, then divide the time available somewhat as follows:
   - If 3-1/2 hours are allowed, that would be 210 minutes. If you have 80 objective-type questions, that would be an average of 2-1/2 minutes per question. Allow yourself no more than 2 minutes per question, or a total of 160 minutes, which will permit about 50 minutes to review.
   - If for the time allotment of 210 minutes there are 7 essay questions to answer, that would average about 30 minutes a question. Give yourself only 25 minutes per question so that you have about 35 minutes to review.

6) The most important instruction is to *read each question* and make sure you know what is wanted. The second most important instruction is to *time yourself properly* so that you answer every question. The third most

important instruction is to *answer every question.* Guess if you have to but include something for each question. Remember that you will receive no credit for a blank and will probably receive some credit if you write something in answer to an essay question. If you guess a letter – say "B" for a multiple-choice question – you may have guessed right. If you leave a blank as an answer to a multiple-choice question, the examiners may respect your feelings but it will not add a point to your score. Some exams may penalize you for wrong answers, so in such cases *only*, you may not want to guess unless you have some basis for your answer.

7) Suggestions
   a. Objective-type questions
      1. Examine the question booklet for proper sequence of pages and questions
      2. Read all instructions carefully
      3. Skip any question which seems too difficult; return to it after all other questions have been answered
      4. Apportion your time properly; do not spend too much time on any single question or group of questions
      5. Note and underline key words – *all, most, fewest, least, best, worst, same, opposite,* etc.
      6. Pay particular attention to negatives
      7. Note unusual option, e.g., unduly long, short, complex, different or similar in content to the body of the question
      8. Observe the use of "hedging" words – *probably, may, most likely,* etc.
      9. Make sure that your answer is put next to the same number as the question
      10. Do not second-guess unless you have good reason to believe the second answer is definitely more correct
      11. Cross out original answer if you decide another answer is more accurate; do not erase until you are ready to hand your paper in
      12. Answer all questions; guess unless instructed otherwise
      13. Leave time for review

   b. Essay questions
      1. Read each question carefully
      2. Determine exactly what is wanted. Underline key words or phrases.
      3. Decide on outline or paragraph answer
      4. Include many different points and elements unless asked to develop any one or two points or elements
      5. Show impartiality by giving pros and cons unless directed to select one side only
      6. Make and write down any assumptions you find necessary to answer the questions
      7. Watch your English, grammar, punctuation and choice of words
      8. Time your answers; don't crowd material

8) Answering the essay question

Most essay questions can be answered by framing the specific response around several key words or ideas. Here are a few such key words or ideas:

M's: manpower, materials, methods, money, management
P's: purpose, program, policy, plan, procedure, practice, problems, pitfalls, personnel, public relations

- a. Six basic steps in handling problems:
    1. Preliminary plan and background development
    2. Collect information, data and facts
    3. Analyze and interpret information, data and facts
    4. Analyze and develop solutions as well as make recommendations
    5. Prepare report and sell recommendations
    6. Install recommendations and follow up effectiveness

- b. Pitfalls to avoid
    1. *Taking things for granted* – A statement of the situation does not necessarily imply that each of the elements is necessarily true; for example, a complaint may be invalid and biased so that all that can be taken for granted is that a complaint has been registered
    2. *Considering only one side of a situation* – Wherever possible, indicate several alternatives and then point out the reasons you selected the best one
    3. *Failing to indicate follow up* – Whenever your answer indicates action on your part, make certain that you will take proper follow-up action to see how successful your recommendations, procedures or actions turn out to be
    4. *Taking too long in answering any single question* – Remember to time your answers properly

IX. AFTER THE TEST

Scoring procedures differ in detail among civil service jurisdictions although the general principles are the same. Whether the papers are hand-scored or graded by machine we have described, they are nearly always graded by number. That is, the person who marks the paper knows only the number – never the name – of the applicant. Not until all the papers have been graded will they be matched with names. If other tests, such as training and experience or oral interview ratings have been given, scores will be combined. Different parts of the examination usually have different weights. For example, the written test might count 60 percent of the final grade, and a rating of training and experience 40 percent. In many jurisdictions, veterans will have a certain number of points added to their grades.

After the final grade has been determined, the names are placed in grade order and an eligible list is established. There are various methods for resolving ties between those who get the same final grade – probably the most common is to place first the name of the person whose application was received first. Job offers are made from the eligible list in the order the names appear on it. You will be notified of your grade and your rank as soon as all these computations have been made. This will be done as rapidly as possible.

People who are found to meet the requirements in the announcement are called "eligibles." Their names are put on a list of eligible candidates. An eligible's chances of getting a job depend on how high he stands on this list and how fast agencies are filling jobs from the list.

When a job is to be filled from a list of eligibles, the agency asks for the names of people on the list of eligibles for that job. When the civil service commission receives this request, it sends to the agency the names of the three people highest on this list. Or, if the job to be filled has specialized requirements, the office sends the agency the names of the top three persons who meet these requirements from the general list.

The appointing officer makes a choice from among the three people whose names were sent to him. If the selected person accepts the appointment, the names of the others are put back on the list to be considered for future openings.

That is the rule in hiring from all kinds of eligible lists, whether they are for typist, carpenter, chemist, or something else. For every vacancy, the appointing officer has his choice of any one of the top three eligibles on the list. This explains why the person whose name is on top of the list sometimes does not get an appointment when some of the persons lower on the list do. If the appointing officer chooses the second or third eligible, the No. 1 eligible does not get a job at once, but stays on the list until he is appointed or the list is terminated.

X. HOW TO PASS THE INTERVIEW TEST

The examination for which you applied requires an oral interview test. You have already taken the written test and you are now being called for the interview test – the final part of the formal examination.

You may think that it is not possible to prepare for an interview test and that there are no procedures to follow during an interview. Our purpose is to point out some things you can do in advance that will help you and some good rules to follow and pitfalls to avoid while you are being interviewed.

What is an interview supposed to test?

The written examination is designed to test the technical knowledge and competence of the candidate; the oral is designed to evaluate intangible qualities, not readily measured otherwise, and to establish a list showing the relative fitness of each candidate – as measured against his competitors – for the position sought. Scoring is not on the basis of "right" and "wrong," but on a sliding scale of values ranging from "not passable" to "outstanding." As a matter of fact, it is possible to achieve a relatively low score without a single "incorrect" answer because of evident weakness in the qualities being measured.

Occasionally, an examination may consist entirely of an oral test – either an individual or a group oral. In such cases, information is sought concerning the technical knowledges and abilities of the candidate, since there has been no written examination for this purpose. More commonly, however, an oral test is used to supplement a written examination.

Who conducts interviews?

The composition of oral boards varies among different jurisdictions. In nearly all, a representative of the personnel department serves as chairman. One of the members of the board may be a representative of the department in which the candidate would work. In some cases, "outside experts" are used, and, frequently, a businessman or some other representative of the general public is asked to serve. Labor and management or other special groups may be represented. The aim is to secure the services of experts in the appropriate field.

However the board is composed, it is a good idea (and not at all improper or unethical) to ascertain in advance of the interview who the members are and what groups they represent. When you are introduced to them, you will have some idea of their backgrounds and interests, and at least you will not stutter and stammer over their names.

What should be done before the interview?

While knowledge about the board members is useful and takes some of the surprise element out of the interview, there is other preparation which is more substantive. It *is* possible to prepare for an oral interview – in several ways:

1) Keep a copy of your application and review it carefully before the interview

This may be the only document before the oral board, and the starting point of the interview. Know what education and experience you have listed there, and the sequence and dates of all of it. Sometimes the board will ask you to review the highlights of your experience for them; you should not have to hem and haw doing it.

2) Study the class specification and the examination announcement

Usually, the oral board has one or both of these to guide them. The qualities, characteristics or knowledges required by the position sought are stated in these documents. They offer valuable clues as to the nature of the oral interview. For example, if the job involves supervisory responsibilities, the announcement will usually indicate that knowledge of modern supervisory methods and the qualifications of the candidate as a supervisor will be tested. If so, you can expect such questions, frequently in the form of a hypothetical situation which you are expected to solve. NEVER go into an oral without knowledge of the duties and responsibilities of the job you seek.

3) Think through each qualification required

Try to visualize the kind of questions you would ask if you were a board member. How well could you answer them? Try especially to appraise your own knowledge and background in each area, *measured against the job sought*, and identify any areas in which you are weak. Be critical and realistic – do not flatter yourself.

4) Do some general reading in areas in which you feel you may be weak

For example, if the job involves supervision and your past experience has NOT, some general reading in supervisory methods and practices, particularly in the field of human relations, might be useful. Do NOT study agency procedures or detailed manuals. The oral board will be testing your understanding and capacity, not your memory.

5) Get a good night's sleep and watch your general health and mental attitude

You will want a clear head at the interview. Take care of a cold or any other minor ailment, and of course, no hangovers.

What should be done on the day of the interview?

Now comes the day of the interview itself. Give yourself plenty of time to get there. Plan to arrive somewhat ahead of the scheduled time, particularly if your appointment is in the fore part of the day. If a previous candidate fails to appear, the board might be ready for you a bit early. By early afternoon an oral board is almost invariably behind schedule if there are many candidates, and you may have to wait.

Take along a book or magazine to read, or your application to review, but leave any extraneous material in the waiting room when you go in for your interview. In any event, relax and compose yourself.

The matter of dress is important. The board is forming impressions about you – from your experience, your manners, your attitude, and your appearance. Give your personal appearance careful attention. Dress your best, but not your flashiest. Choose conservative, appropriate clothing, and be sure it is immaculate. This is a business interview, and your appearance should indicate that you regard it as such. Besides, being well groomed and properly dressed will help boost your confidence.

Sooner or later, someone will call your name and escort you into the interview room. *This is it.* From here on you are on your own. It is too late for any more preparation. But remember, you asked for this opportunity to prove your fitness, and you are here because your request was granted.

What happens when you go in?

The usual sequence of events will be as follows: The clerk (who is often the board stenographer) will introduce you to the chairman of the oral board, who will introduce you to the other members of the board. Acknowledge the introductions before you sit down. Do not be surprised if you find a microphone facing you or a stenotypist sitting by. Oral interviews are usually recorded in the event of an appeal or other review.

Usually the chairman of the board will open the interview by reviewing the highlights of your education and work experience from your application – primarily for the benefit of the other members of the board, as well as to get the material into the record. Do not interrupt or comment unless there is an error or significant misinterpretation; if that is the case, do not hesitate. But do not quibble about insignificant matters. Also, he will usually ask you some question about your education, experience or your present job – partly to get you to start talking and to establish the interviewing "rapport." He may start the actual questioning, or turn it over to one of the other members. Frequently, each member undertakes the questioning on a particular area, one in which he is perhaps most competent, so you can expect each member to participate in the examination. Because time is limited, you may also expect some rather abrupt switches in the direction the questioning takes, so do not be upset by it. Normally, a board member will not pursue a single line of questioning unless he discovers a particular strength or weakness.

After each member has participated, the chairman will usually ask whether any member has any further questions, then will ask you if you have anything you wish to add. Unless you are expecting this question, it may floor you. Worse, it may start you off on an extended, extemporaneous speech. The board is not usually seeking more information. The question is principally to offer you a last opportunity to present further qualifications or to indicate that you have nothing to add. So, if you feel that a significant qualification or characteristic has been overlooked, it is proper to point it out in a sentence or so. Do not compliment the board on the thoroughness of their examination – they have been sketchy, and you know it. If you wish, merely say, "No thank you, I have nothing further to add." This is a point where you can "talk yourself out" of a good impression or fail to present an important bit of information. Remember, *you close the interview yourself.*

The chairman will then say, "That is all, Mr. _____, thank you." Do not be startled; the interview is over, and quicker than you think. Thank him, gather your belongings and take your leave. Save your sigh of relief for the other side of the door.

How to put your best foot forward

Throughout this entire process, you may feel that the board individually and collectively is trying to pierce your defenses, seek out your hidden weaknesses and embarrass and confuse you. Actually, this is not true. They are obliged to make an appraisal of your qualifications for the job you are seeking, and they want to see you in your best light. Remember, they must interview all candidates and a non-cooperative candidate may become a failure in spite of their best efforts to bring out his qualifications. Here are 15 suggestions that will help you:

1) Be natural – Keep your attitude confident, not cocky

If you are not confident that you can do the job, do not expect the board to be. Do not apologize for your weaknesses, try to bring out your strong points. The board is interested in a positive, not negative, presentation. Cockiness will antagonize any board member and make him wonder if you are covering up a weakness by a false show of strength.

2) Get comfortable, but don't lounge or sprawl

Sit erectly but not stiffly. A careless posture may lead the board to conclude that you are careless in other things, or at least that you are not impressed by the importance of the occasion. Either conclusion is natural, even if incorrect. Do not fuss with your clothing, a pencil or an ashtray. Your hands may occasionally be useful to emphasize a point; do not let them become a point of distraction.

3) Do not wisecrack or make small talk

This is a serious situation, and your attitude should show that you consider it as such. Further, the time of the board is limited – they do not want to waste it, and neither should you.

4) Do not exaggerate your experience or abilities

In the first place, from information in the application or other interviews and sources, the board may know more about you than you think. Secondly, you probably will not get away with it. An experienced board is rather adept at spotting such a situation, so do not take the chance.

5) If you know a board member, do not make a point of it, yet do not hide it

Certainly you are not fooling him, and probably not the other members of the board. Do not try to take advantage of your acquaintanceship – it will probably do you little good.

6) Do not dominate the interview

Let the board do that. They will give you the clues – do not assume that you have to do all the talking. Realize that the board has a number of questions to ask you, and do not try to take up all the interview time by showing off your extensive knowledge of the answer to the first one.

7) Be attentive

You only have 20 minutes or so, and you should keep your attention at its sharpest throughout. When a member is addressing a problem or question to you, give him your undivided attention. Address your reply principally to him, but do not exclude the other board members.

8) Do not interrupt
A board member may be stating a problem for you to analyze. He will ask you a question when the time comes. Let him state the problem, and wait for the question.

9) Make sure you understand the question
Do not try to answer until you are sure what the question is. If it is not clear, restate it in your own words or ask the board member to clarify it for you. However, do not haggle about minor elements.

10) Reply promptly but not hastily
A common entry on oral board rating sheets is "candidate responded readily," or "candidate hesitated in replies." Respond as promptly and quickly as you can, but do not jump to a hasty, ill-considered answer.

11) Do not be peremptory in your answers
A brief answer is proper – but do not fire your answer back. That is a losing game from your point of view. The board member can probably ask questions much faster than you can answer them.

12) Do not try to create the answer you think the board member wants
He is interested in what kind of mind you have and how it works – not in playing games. Furthermore, he can usually spot this practice and will actually grade you down on it.

13) Do not switch sides in your reply merely to agree with a board member
Frequently, a member will take a contrary position merely to draw you out and to see if you are willing and able to defend your point of view. Do not start a debate, yet do not surrender a good position. If a position is worth taking, it is worth defending.

14) Do not be afraid to admit an error in judgment if you are shown to be wrong
The board knows that you are forced to reply without any opportunity for careful consideration. Your answer may be demonstrably wrong. If so, admit it and get on with the interview.

15) Do not dwell at length on your present job
The opening question may relate to your present assignment. Answer the question but do not go into an extended discussion. You are being examined for a *new* job, not your present one. As a matter of fact, try to phrase ALL your answers in terms of the job for which you are being examined.

Basis of Rating

Probably you will forget most of these "do's" and "don'ts" when you walk into the oral interview room. Even remembering them all will not ensure you a passing grade. Perhaps you did not have the qualifications in the first place. But remembering them will help you to put your best foot forward, without treading on the toes of the board members.

Rumor and popular opinion to the contrary notwithstanding, an oral board wants you to make the best appearance possible. They know you are under pressure – but they also want to see how you respond to it as a guide to what your reaction would be under the pressures of the job you seek. They will be influenced by the degree of poise you display, the personal traits you show and the manner in which you respond.

EXAMINATION SECTION

EXAMINATION SECTION
TEST 1

DIRECTIONS: Each question or incomplete statement is followed by several suggested answers or completions. Select the one that BEST answers the question or completes the statement. *PRINT THE LETTER OF THE CORRECT ANSWER IN THE SPACE AT THE RIGHT.*

1. A television receiver has a GREATER inherent fire hazard than a conventional radio receiver because
    A. of greater electrical leakage
    B. cabinets are inadequately ventilated
    C. higher voltage is used in the system
    D. they are operated for longer periods of time
    E. the coaxial cable lead-in is covered with a highly flammable coating

    1.___

2. Of the following, the MOST frequent factor contributing to conflagrations in the United States and Canada in the last 25 years has been
    A. high winds
    B. lack of exposure protection
    C. delayed alarms
    D. congestion of hazardous occupancies
    E. inadequate water distribution system

    2.___

3. If, upon reinspection of a plant which has 30 days to comply with a previous order, you find that the order has not been completely obeyed but that some work has taken place, you SHOULD
    A. report to proper authorities to obtain legal action
    B. assume the delay is unavoidable and check again in 30 days
    C. inform the person in charge that a 10-day extension will be granted and that legal action will be taken if the order has not been followed
    D. issue a summons for failure to comply
    E. none of the above

    3.___

4. An analysis of loss records in one city showed that one-third of the total loss in building fires was in residence buildings and that, of the total loss in such buildings, in the year under study, nearly 80 percent was in multiple dwelling buildings.
The one of the following courses of action for the Fire Department which should be taken IMMEDIATELY on the basis of this report is to
    A. relocate companies
    B. recommend sprinkler protection for multiple dwellings
    C. institute special training fighting multiple dwelling fires
    D. reduce the protection given to other than multiple dwelling residences
    E. inspect multiple dwellings more thoroughly

    4.___

5. It is good practice to so install heating devices that under conditions of maximum heat (long-continued exposure) they will not cause the temperature of exposed woodwork to exceed 160°F.
This practice is
   A. *correct*, because of the possibility that wood and other combustible materials, after long-continued exposure to relatively moderate heat, may ignite at temperatures far below their usual ignition temperatures
   B. *not correct*, because no wood in ordinary use will ignite at a temperature of less than 400°F and, consequently, the requirement is needlessly severe
   C. *correct*, because oxidation proceeds much more rapidly at higher temperatures
   D. *not correct*, because oxidation proceeds much more slowly at higher temperatures
   E. *correct*, because under prolonged heating the temperature of the air in the room will build up until the ignition point is reached unless the applied temperature is kept sufficiently low

6. Analysis of the causes of fires is important, as only by knowing the causes of fires is it possible to effectively prevent fire.
An analysis of fires in rooms used for spraying flammable paints and finishes has shown that the MOST important of the following causes is
   A. smoking by employees
   B. defective electrical equipment
   C. spontaneous ignition of paint deposits, rubbish, and wiping rags
   D. static electricity resulting from friction
   E. cutting and welding operations

7. The flammability or combustibility of radioactive materials has little or no direct effect on the fire hazard of a laboratory PRIMARILY because
   A. the unusual structural characteristics of such a laboratory serve to limit possible fire spread from such hazards
   B. water or water spray are effective on most radioactive substances
   C. the quantities of such material in any one laboratory are usually small
   D. laboratory fire prevention and firefighting facilities usually exceed maximum fire hazards
   E. such materials are inherently of a low order of combustibility

8. Comparison of the burning qualities of foam rubber and cotton mattresses shows that GENERALLY
   A. a cotton mattress burns faster but cooler
   B. a foam rubber mattress burns slower but hotter

C. a foam rubber mattress burns faster and hotter
D. a cotton mattress burns faster and hotter
E. the potential fire hazard of a foam rubber mattress is higher

9. During Christmas and other holiday shopping seasons, it is required that frequent inspections shall be made of department stores at irregular intervals.
Of the following, the MOST important reason for this inspection procedure is to
A. prevent unnecessary interference with store operations
B. check characteristic holiday operations
C. permit more frequent and thorough coverage of the stores in question
D. avoid delay in urgent fire operations
E. permit more flexible scheduling of inspection

10. The fire load computation of a building indicates, for the most part, the
A. risk of a fire breaking out
B. rate at which a fire is likely to grow
C. combustibility of the various parts of the building rather than its contents
D. amount of combustibles and the method of protection
E. maximum fire stress to which the building might be subjected

11. It is far more important that escape routes from multi-story buildings should be protected against smoke and hot gases than from direct flame or heat.
This statement is
A. *not correct*; resistive construction is likely to be smoke-resistive as well
B. *correct*; adequate means for ventilation is essential to prevent cutting off escape routes
C. *not correct*; unless corridors and escape stairs are constructed of fire resistive materials, progress of fire cannot be blocked
D. *correct*; unless properly protected from smoke and hot gases, escape stairs would be unusable by occupants
E. *not correct*; unless properly protected against direct flame or heat, escape routes cannot resist smoke or hot gases

12. The MINIMUM width of exit usually required for a single file of persons is MOST NEARLY _____ inches.
A. 15-17   B. 18-20   C. 21-23
D. 24-27   E. 27-30

13. The MOST pronounced method of reducing the fire and life hazards in public buildings is by
A. ample exits of any type
B. ample stairways inside the buildings

    C. the use of exit signs and panic locks
    D. fire-resisting construction suitable for the occupancy
    E. installing fire extinguishers in every hallway

14. From all viewpoints, the MOST hazardous materials that could be stored, constituting a life as well as a fire hazard, would be
    A. second-hand niter bags
    B. used motor vehicles
    C. loose or baled vegetable fibers
    D. pyroxylin and pyroxylin plastic products
    E. foam rubber mattresses

15. The CHIEF fire hazard of welding and cutting operations is
    A. flames of the torch igniting nearby material
    B. broken hose line
    C. flying sparks
    D. backfiring of torch
    E. tank explosion

16. Of the following items associated with motion picture theatres, the PRIMARY hazard is
    A. misuse of electricity   B. heating defects
    C. smoking and matches   D. projection booth fires
    E. improperly lit exits

17. The MOST hazardous method of fumigation is by the use of
    A. heat (125°F)
    B. carbon tetrachloride mixture with flammable fumigant
    C. carbon dioxide mixture with flammable fumigant
    D. carbon bisulphide
    E. carbon monoxide

18. The combined use of inspections, periodic reports of activities, follow-up procedures, special reports from subordinates, and a rating system comprise a system of
    A. coordination   B. command
    C. control   D. representation
    E. on-the-job training

19. What should be provided in air conditioning ducts to PREVENT the spread of fire and smoke through a property?
    A. Automatic dampers   B. Intake screens
    C. Steel wool air filters   D. Heat actuated devices
    E. Halon extinguishers

20. The OUTSTANDING fire hazard of boarding and rooming houses is
    A. misuse of electricity   B. smoking and matches
    C. heating defects   D. incendiary
    E. kitchen fires

21. The SIMPLEST and MOST feasible method of avoiding the overheating of woodwork near any high temperature heating appliance is by
    A. filling the intervening space with insulating material
    B. covering the woodwork with sheet metal
    C. providing an air space between the woodwork and the appliance
    D. covering the woodwork with asbestos sheets
    E. painting the woodwork with varnish

22. The PRINCIPLE source of fire hazard in connection with heating equipment in mercantile buildings comes from
    A. defective wiring
    B. insufficient clearance from combustible materials
    C. the storage and handling of fuel
    D. defective motors
    E. none of the above

23. More ink has been spilled on the item of smoking as a cause of fire than on any other, but the total result has been negligible.
    This situation is BEST accounted for by the fact that
    A. smoking is generally an automatic act performed unthinkingly
    B. truly effective facilities for elimination of smoking hazards are exceedingly cumbersome or expensive
    C. most people regard smoking as a personal prerogative and resent control measures
    D. smoking is practiced by many individuals with defective intelligence and social attitudes
    E. individual behavior cannot be controlled

24. There are two basic factors in assessing building construction from the fire prevention standpoint. One is the combustibility of materials.
    The other is
    A. extinguishment facilities
    B. excess structural strength
    C. ventilation control
    D. limitation of fire spread
    E. means of access and egress

25. The LEAST accurate statement concerning the protection of openings in walls and partitions is:
    A. Protection of wall openings may prevent either the horizontal or the vertical spread of fire
    B. The general features of a building have no bearing on the extent to which such protection is necessary
    C. The protection secured by fire doors and fire windows cannot be better than the fire resistant value of the walls
    D. Good solid walls are preferable to those with fire doors in restricting the spread of fire
    E. Sprinkler systems may provide adequate protection

26. The one of the following which is NOT included among the six categories in which all structures are classified by the Administrative Code with respect to type of construction is _____ structures.
    A. heavy timber   B. metal   C. wood frame
    D. fire-resistant E. fireproof

27. All storage tanks, comprising or forming a part of an oil storage plant, shall be buried so that the tops thereof shall be a distance below the grade level of AT LEAST
    A. 1'   B. 2'   C. 3'   D. 4'   E. 6'

28. According to the Administrative Code, a Class B refrigeration system is one
   A. capable of less than 15 tons capacity
   B. containing not more than 20 lbs. of refrigerant
   C. capable of less than 30 tons capacity
   D. containing 1000 pounds or over of refrigerant
   E. capable of 40 tons capacity or over

29. According to the Administrative Code, it shall be unlawful to transport or store guncotton EXCEPT in
   A. strong wooden cases lined with liquid-proof paper
   B. strong wooden cases
   C. carboys so tinted as to exclude light
   D. water-tight metal vessels
   E. aluminum or other non-tarnishing metal

30. One purpose of building inspections is to enable the Fire Department to plan its operations before a fire starts.
   This statement is
   A. *incorrect*; no two fires are alike
   B. *correct*; many firefighting problems can be anticipated
   C. *incorrect*; fires should be prevented, not extinguished
   D. *correct*; the Fire Department should have detailed plans for every possible emergency
   E. *incorrect*; fires are not predictable

KEY (CORRECT ANSWERS)

1. C	11. D	21. C
2. A	12. C	22. B
3. A	13. D	23. A
4. E	14. D	24. D
5. A	15. C	25. B
6. C	16. D	26. D
7. C	17. D	27. B
8. C	18. C	28. C
9. B	19. A	29. D
10. E	20. C	30. B

TEST 2

DIRECTIONS: Each question or incomplete statement is followed by several suggested answers or completions. Select the one that BEST answers the question or completes the statement. *PRINT THE LETTER OF THE CORRECT ANSWER IN THE SPACE AT THE RIGHT.*

1. According to the Fire Prevention Code, an essential oil is defined as an oil
   A. needed to provide the viscosity of a given grade of oil
   B. derived from animal life and not from mineral sources
   C. which has low volatility at room temperature
   D. used for flavoring or perfuming purposes
   E. required as the base of lubricating compounds

   1.___

2. According to the Fire Prevention Code, it shall be UNLAWFUL to sell or deliver for use
   A. sticks or cartridges of explosives which are packed so as to lie on their sides
   B. any explosive except in original and unbroken packages
   C. dynamite in cases of 25 and 50 lbs.
   D. nitroglycerine in liquid form under any circumstances
   E. any explosives packed in quantities in excess of 50 lbs.

   2.___

3. The Fire Prevention Code requires that a storage garage containing more than four motor vehicles shall be continuously under the supervision of one or more persons, each holding a certificate of fitness.
   The MAXIMUM number of such certificated persons required for any garage shall be
   A. 7   B. 6   C. 5   D. 4   E. 3

   3.___

4. According to the annual report statistics for the last years, the floor of multiple dwellings where fires started MOST frequently was the
   A. cellar   B. 1st floor   C. 2nd floor
   D. 3rd floor   E. roof

   4.___

5. You are assigned to inspect buildings for fire hazards. The one of the following MOST appropriately used for fire-retardant coating of wood is
   A. varnish   B. shellac   C. wood stain
   D. lacquer   E. white wash

   5.___

6. An officer taking some clothing to a dry cleaner in his neighborhood noticed that inflammable cleaning fluid was stored in a way which created a fire hazard. The officer called this to the attention of the proprietor, explaining the danger involved.

   6.___

This method of handling the situation was
- A. *bad*; the officer should not have interfered in a matter which was not his responsibility
- B. *good*; the proprietor would probably remove the hazard and be more careful in the future
- C. *bad*; the officer should have reported the situation to the fire inspector's office without saying anything to the proprietor
- D. *good*; since the officer was a customer, he should treat the proprietor more leniently than he would treat other violators
- E. *bad*; the officer should have ordered the proprietor to remove the violation immediately and issued a summons

7. Automobile fires are caused MOST frequently by
   - A. overheating of the motor
   - B. gasoline explosion
   - C. defective carburetor
   - D. defective or overheated brakes
   - E. faulty ignition wiring

8. The PRINCIPAL fire hazard in connection with heating equipment in mercantile buildings comes from
   - A. failure to operate and clean equipment properly
   - B. insufficient clearance from combustible material
   - C. use of improper types or grades of fuel
   - D. defective flues
   - E. exposed wiring in heating controls

9. Supermarket fires have in common the fact that MOST fires occur in the
   - A. utility area
   - B. sales area
   - C. basement storage area
   - D. check-out and packaging area
   - E. shelves containing paper products

10. Of the following, the LEAST accurate statement concerning Field Violation Cards is that
    - A. when all the violations listed on a Field Violation Card have been complied with, such card shall be placed in the Occupancy Folder
    - B. not more than two Minor Violation Orders shall be recorded on any one card
    - C. not more than two Major Violation Orders shall be recorded on any one card
    - D. when the space on both sides is completely used for entries, such card is placed on file in the Occupancy Folder
    - E. when subsequent violations are found for a building which previously complied with violations found, the additional entries shall be made on the same Field Violation Card

11. Of the following statements concerning coal storage, the one that is ACCEPTABLE is:
    A. Coal for storage should preferably be deposited in horizontal layers
    B. Alternate wetting and drying will prevent development of heat in the pile
    C. The desirable height of a properly stored coal pile is 25 to 30 feet
    D. Storage of mixed sizes of coal together will reduce spontaneous ignition to a minimum
    E. Standing timbers should be placed in coal piles to provide air access and circulation

12. The Multiple Dwelling Law provides that, in every multiple dwelling erected after April 18, 1929, every stair, fire stair, and fire tower beyond a specified width shall be provided with a handrail on each side.
    This specified width is
    A. 3'2"   B. 3'8"   C. 4'2"   D. 4'10"   E. 5'6"

13. The one of the following for which the Official Action Guide provides that a permit is required for storage, regardless of quantity and purpose, is
    A. shale oil   B. heavy lubricating oil
    C. machine oil   D. kerosene
    E. illuminating oil

Questions 14-16.

DIRECTIONS: Questions 14 through 16, inclusive, are to be answered on the basis of the following paragraph.

A flameproof fabric is defined as one which, when exposed to small sources of ignition, such as sparks or smoldering cigarettes, does not burn beyond the vicinity of the source of ignition. Cotton fabrics are the materials commonly used that are considered most hazardous. Other materials, such as acetate rayons and linens, are somewhat less hazardous, and woolens and some natural silk fabrics, even when untreated, are about equal to the average treated cotton fabric insofar as flame spread and ease of ignition are concerned. The method of application is to immerse the fabric in a flame-proofing solution. The container used must be large enough so that all the fabric is thoroughly wet and there are no folds which the solution does not penetrate.

14. According to the above paragraph, a flameproof fabric is one which
    A. is unaffected by heat and smoke
    B. resists the spread of flames when ignited
    C. burns with a cold flame
    D. cannot be ignited by sparks or cigarettes
    E. may smolder but cannot burn

15. According to the above paragraph, woolen fabrics which have not been flameproofed are as likely to catch fire as _____ fabrics.
    A. treated silk   B. treated acetate rayon
    C. untreated linen   D. untreated synthetic
    E. treated cotton

16. In the method described above, the flameproofing solution is BEST applied to the fabric by _____ the fabric.
    A. sponging   B. spraying   C. dipping
    D. brushing   E. sprinkling

17. The daily peak time for the number of fires in the city, in general,
    A. varies from day to day
    B. is about 9 A.M.
    C. is at about 5 P.M.
    D. is at about 1 A.M.
    E. varies from season to season

18. According to the Multiple Dwelling Law, a part of a building is *fire-retarded* if it is protected against fire in an approved manner with materials of fire-resistive ratings of AT LEAST _____ hour(s).
    A. one   B. two   C. three   D. four   E. five

19. The Multiple Dwelling Law permits the conduct of business in any multiple dwelling EXCEPT that
    A. no space in a non-fireproof multiple dwelling may be used for a bakery or business where fat is boiled under any condition
    B. the number of persons employed in manufacturing enterprises in multiple dwellings shall be limited to a maximum of seven persons
    C. exits of the dwelling portion and the business space may be common if the number of persons employed is limited to ten persons or less
    D. when the ground story of any non-fireproof multiple dwelling is extended for business purposes, the underside of the roof of such extension shall be fire-retarded if there are fire escapes above such extension
    E. there shall be no manufacturing business conducted above the second floor of any non-fireproof multiple dwelling

20. According to the Building Code, a sprinkler system is NOT required in
    A. garages in cellars of multiple dwellings if area is less than 5,000 square feet
    B. dressing rooms and stage of auditoriums of large public high schools where seating capacity is less than 1,500
    C. furnished rooms of converted non-fireproof multiple dwellings if the public hall has sprinkler protection

D. non-fireproof lodging houses if equipped with an automatic, closed-circuit fire alarm system
E. department stores if each floor does not exceed 10,000 square feet

21. The Building Code requires that in all newly constructed loft buildings used for mercantile purposes,
    A. 8 inch standpipe risers shall be installed in buildings 150 feet or more in height
    B. standpipes be installed if 75 feet in height or over
    C. the minimum size of standpipe riser in a building 100 feet high be at least 3 inches
    D. when a standpipe is required, no point on a floor be more than 75 feet from a riser
    E. multiple standpipe risers may not be cross-connected

22. The proscenium of a theatre is MOST closely associated with the
    A. stage
    B. special entrance for scenery
    C. street entrance and exit
    D. passageways to boxes
    E. balcony arch over the orchestra section

23. The MAXIMUM quantity of kerosene fuel oil that may be stored for heating and cooking use without a permit from the Fire Commissioner is _____ gallons.
    A. 10   B. 25   C. 50   D. 100   E. 150

24. An ACCEPTABLE method of absorbing waste oils in a dry cleaning establishment is, according to the Fire Prevention Code,
    A. a quantity of sand spread on the floor
    B. use of thin asbestos fibre flooring
    C. non-combustible cloth on the floor
    D. diatomaceous earth or equivalent absorbent material spread on the floor
    E. woven glass fibre mats

25. Suppose you are making an inspection of a factory. During the inspection, the factory manager asks you a technical question which you cannot answer.
    Of the following, the BEST procedure for you to follow is to
    A. tell him you are not there to answer his questions but to make an inspection
    B. guess at the answer so that he won't doubt your competency
    C. tell him you don't know the answer but that you will look it up and notify him
    D. give him the title of a textbook that probably would contain the information
    E. change the subject by asking him a question

26. While performing building inspections, a fireman finds a janitor in the basement checking for a gas leak by holding a lighted match to the gas pipes.
    Of the following, the fireman's FIRST action should be to
    A. reprimand the janitor for endangering life and property
    B. explain the hazards of this action to the janitor
    C. report the janitor to his superior as incompetent
    D. tell the janitor to put out the match
    E. issue a summons for this action

27. According to the Administrative Code, a refrigerant is defined as the chemical agent used to produce refrigeration other than
    A. brine
    B. a chemical of the hydrocarbon clan
    C. the compressor
    D. methyl bromide
    E. ammonia

28. The Administrative Code defines as a combustible mixture any substance which, when tested in a Tagliabue open cup tester, emits an inflammable vapor at temperatures
    A. below 100°F   B. above 300°F
    C. between 100°F and 300°F   D. below 125°F
    E. above 125°F

29. A partially filled gasoline drum is a more dangerous fire hazard than a full one.
    Of the following, the BEST justification for this statement is that
    A. a partially filled gasoline drum contains relatively little air
    B. gasoline is difficult to ignite
    C. when a gasoline drum is full, the gasoline is more explosive
    D. gasoline vapors are more explosive than gasoline itself
    E. air is not combustible

30. The tendency of this substance to spontaneous heating is very slight. It is usually shipped in bulk. This substance should be kept dry, and storing or loading in hot wet piles should be avoided.
    This description applies MOST closely to
    A. metal powder   B. soft coal   C. charcoal
    D. scrap film   E. jute

KEY (CORRECT ANSWERS)

1. D	11. A	21. B
2. B	12. B	22. A
3. E	13. A	23. A
4. A	14. B	24. A
5. E	15. E	25. C
6. B	16. C	26. D
7. E	17. C	27. A
8. B	18. A	28. C
9. A	19. E	29. D
10. E	20. E	30. E

TEST 3

DIRECTIONS: Each question or incomplete statement is followed by several suggested answers or completions. Select the one that BEST answers the question or completes the statement. *PRINT THE LETTER OF THE CORRECT ANSWER IN THE SPACE AT THE RIGHT.*

1. An inspector is denied access to a building by the building manager after presenting his identification. Of the following actions, it would be MOST appropriate for the captain to
    A. post an official notice of inspection on the premises
    B. notify the enforcement unit of the division of fire prevention
    C. give orders to have three routine inspections of premises made before taking special measures to gain access
    D. contact the building owner by telephone to request access

1.___

Questions 2-5.

DIRECTIONS: Questions 2 through 5 are to be answered on the basis of the information given in the following paragraph.

    Old buildings are liable to possess a special degree of fire risk merely because they are old. Outmoded electrical wiring systems and installation of new heating appliances for which the building was not designed may contribute to the increased hazard. Old buildings have often been altered many times; parts of the structure may antedate building codes; dangerous defects may have been covered up. On the average, old buildings contain more lumber than comparable new buildings which, in itself, makes old buildings more susceptible to fire. It is not true, though, that sound lumber in old buildings is drier than new lumber. Moisture content of lumber varies with that of the atmosphere to which it is exposed.

2. According to the above paragraph, old buildings present a special fire hazard CHIEFLY because of the
    A. poor planning of the buildings when first designed
    B. haphazard alteration of the buildings
    C. failure to replace worn out equipment
    D. inadequate enforcement of the building codes

2.___

3. We may conclude from the above paragraph that lumber
    A. should not be used in buildings unless absolutely necessary
    B. should not be used near electrical equipment

3.___

C. is more inflammable than newer types of building
   materials
D. tends to lose its moisture at a constant rate

4. According to the above paragraph, the amount of moisture   4.___
   in the wooden parts of a building depends upon the
   A. age of the building
   B. moisture in the surrounding air
   C. type of heating equipment used in the building
   D. quality of lumber used

5. In regard to building codes, the above paragraph implies   5.___
   that
   A. old buildings are exempt from the provisions of
      building codes
   B. some buildings now in use were built before building
      codes were adopted
   C. building codes usually don't cover electrical wiring
      systems
   D. building codes generally are inadequate

6. According to Department Regulations, the *Monthly Statis-*   6.___
   tical Report - Field Inspection Activity should include
   company field inspection duty of all
   A. types
   B. types except re-inspection duty on violation orders
   C. types except surveillance inspection duty
   D. types except inspectional duty relative to complaints

7. During field inspection of a building containing an   7.___
   automatic sprinkler system, you note that the shut-off
   valves are located where they are not readily accessible.
   The one of the following procedures to follow in this
   situation, according to department regulations, is to
   A. write an order to the owner or occupant requiring
      correction of the physical defect
   B. require no action by the owner or occupant but make
      special note of the valve location in the building
      record file
   C. bring to the attention of the owner or occupant the
      potential water damage hazard inherent in this
      situation
   D. write an order to the owner or occupant for a sign
      indicating valve location

8. The difficulties encountered in fighting fire in the   8.___
   cellar of a pool supply occupancy were compounded by bulk
   storage of calcium hypochlorite.
   This bleaching and sanitizing agent is LEAST likely to
   A. be unstable and highly combustible when finely divided
   B. form a mixture that spontaneously bursts into flame
      on contact with oxidizable material
   C. decompose when involved in fire, by liberating oxygen
      and intensifying the fire
   D. have an increased fire and explosion potential when
      pre-mixed with algaecides and fungicides as an all-
      purpose water treatment

9. Acetylene is a particularly hazardous flammable gas because, in addition to its flammability, it is reactive and unstable. Consequently, its storage and handling in some respects differs from other flammable gases.
The following statements may be pertinent to acetylene and its storage:
   I. Acetylene is not toxic but can have an anesthetic effect
   II. Copper must be avoided in most acetylene piping and equipment
   III. Acetylene gas can explode if subjected to more than 15 psi
Which one of the following choices lists only those of the abovementioned statements that are generally CORRECT?
   A. I, II   B. II, III   C. I, III   D. I, II, III

10. Before leaving quarters to perform apparatus field inspection duty (AFID) at a hospital, a company officer holds a drill on institutional fire safety.
It would be MOST appropriate for the officer to tell the members that the MAJORITY of fires in hospitals generally occur in
   A. storage rooms   B. lounges
   C. patients' rooms   D. corridors

11. Special fire hazards in industry are sometimes diminished by automatic carbon dioxide fixed-pipe extinguishing systems. While difficult to check an existing system for compliance with design and installation standards, certain of the following conditions can be noted during a building inspection to determine whether it is apparently operative and in good order:
   I. Have cylinders been weighed within the past five years and is there a visible record of such weighing?
   II. Are automatic-closing doors and shutters unobstructed and free to close upon actuation?
   III. Are there means accessible during a fire of manually actuating the system?
Which of the following choices contains only those of the above conditions that are generally VALID?
   A. I, II   B. II, III   C. I, III   D. I, II, III

12. A considerable number of serious burn injuries and fatalities result from fires involving clothing being worn. The following may or may not be correct statements concerning Fire Department experience gained from such fires:
   I. Cotton and rayon have proved to be relatively non-flammable fibers
   II. Nylon and acetate melt and liquefy under fire exposure, thereby tending to aggravate the severity of burn injuries
   III. Victims of clothing fires are more likely to be persons over 60 years of age than children under 10

Which of the following choices contains only those of the above-mentioned statements that are generally CORRECT?
A. I, II   B. I, III   C. II, III   D. I, II, III

13. Some communities have a program for inspecting dwellings, conducted as a courtesy and service to householders.
The USUAL effect of a dwelling-house inspection campaign is
    A. annoyance on the part of homeowners and their refusal to admit firemen
    B. anticipation of firemen's visits by cleaning up before their arrival
    C. avoidance of major problems found by firemen and their stressing instead the easily corrected conditions
    D. embarrassment of both firemen and homeowners by the procedure and their seeking premature termination of the visit

14. Of the following agents for transferring flammable and combustible liquids, the BEST one is
    A. air pressure
    B. hydraulic or inert gas
    C. straight gravity discharge systems
    D. positive displacement pumps

15. The effect of applying wallpaper to a new interior finish surface on the flame propagation characteristics of that surface is GENERALLY considered
    A. minimal   B. moderate
    C. considerable   D. severe

16. While you are on apparatus field inspection duty, one of your members reports that he has issued an order to a building owner to remedy a violation forthwith. The member states that the owner seems agitated and hostile and refuses to correct the condition. You decide to speak to the owner yourself.
In discussing this situation with the owner, it is MOST advisable for you to
    A. inform the owner firmly but bluntly that he is incorrect in insisting the condition does not require correction
    B. try to convince the owner that you are an expert in this area and that your knowledge should not be questioned
    C. express an appropriate degree of anger at the owner's refusal to correct an unsafe condition
    D. stick to discussion of the specific violation and avoid trying to convince the owner of the importance of correcting all fire hazards

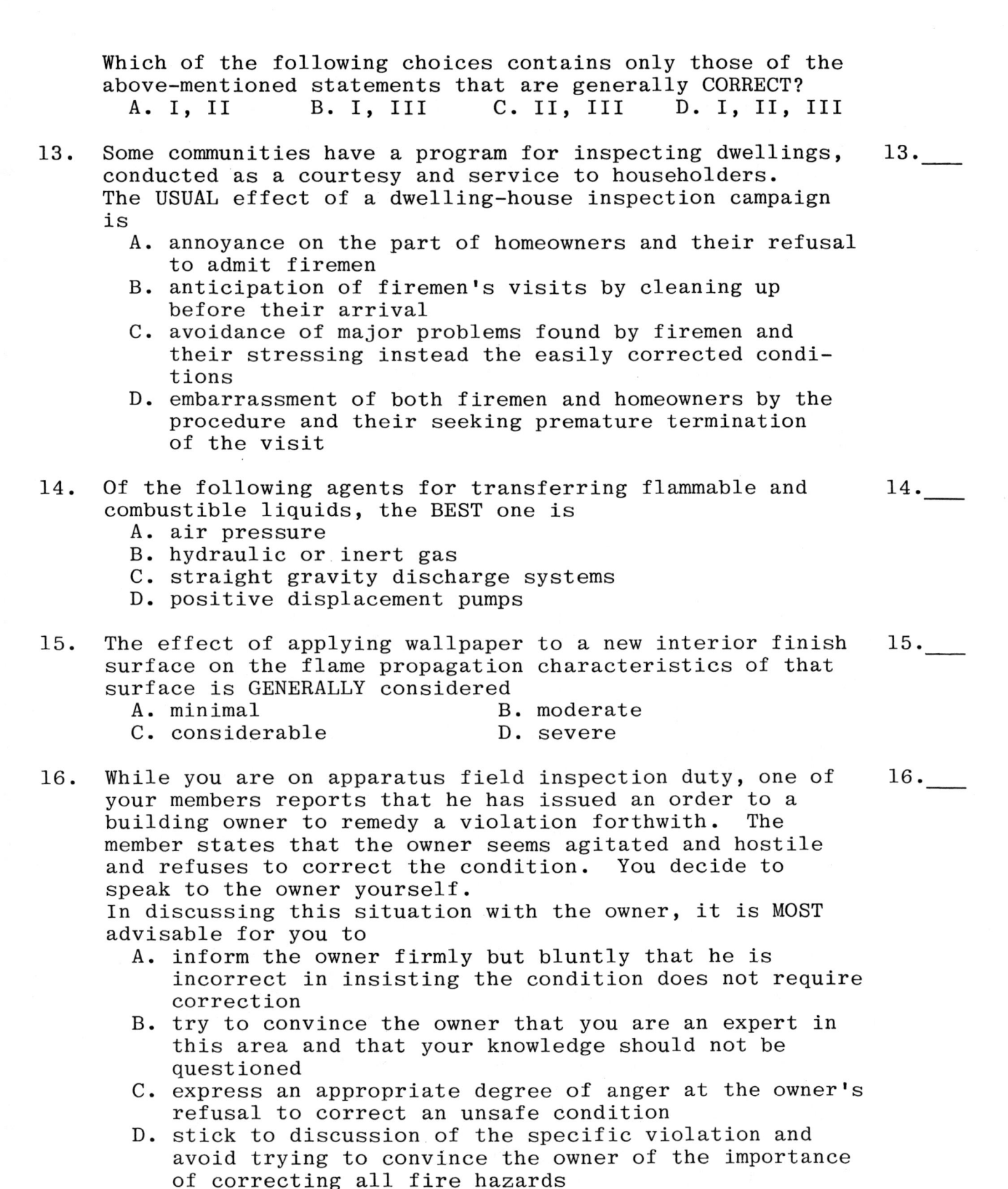

17. Experience with the city fire prevention program GENERALLY demonstrates that
    A. fires have increased in the public areas of ghetto multiple dwellings despite intensive inspections
    B. inspections are ineffective in both loft buildings and ghetto multiple dwellings
    C. the extensive educational program in the schools in the 1950's resulted in decreases in the number of fires and false alarms when the children reached adulthood
    D. fires have increased in the living areas of ghetto multiple dwellings

18. It is common to find self-closing doors kept open with wooden wedges or other fastenings. To eliminate such unsafe hazards, hooks, fitted with fusible links, have been designed to hold the doors open.
    GENERALLY, these hooks are
    A. *desirable*, if placed low enough for convenient use
    B. *undesirable*, unless placed behind doors, where they would not be subject to damage
    C. *desirable*, if used only on stair and corridor doors
    D. *undesirable* under practically all conditions

19. While supervising an inspection of a commercial building, an officer notices some wooden packing cases resting against a steam riser. He advises the owner to move the stock at least 12 inches away from the riser to permit air to circulate.
    This advice GENERALLY is
    A. *proper*; however, a clearance of 36 inches should have been suggested
    B. *improper*; steam risers do not reach the ignition temperature of wood
    C. *proper*; standard practice uses a rise of 90°F above room temperature as the maximum permissible temperature on surrounding woodwork
    D. *improper*; the air space suggested may permit hidden fire to travel behind the stock

20. Realistic fire tests to determine the actual burning characteristics of several rigid foam plastic wall and roof assemblies have been conducted within recent years. Of the following conclusions, the one BEST supported by this research is that
    A. low flame spread, rigid polystyrene foam, encased in aluminum skins, required automatic sprinkler protection for satisfactory performance under fire conditions
    B. low flame spread, rigid polyurethane foam, encased in aluminum skins, required automatic sprinkler protection for satisfactory performance under fire conditions

C. rigid, foamed polyurethane products produce minimum fire contribution when sprayed on walls
D. materials with a small-scale flame spread rating of 25 are practically self-extinguishing

21. At a neighborhood community organization meeting and discussion on *Fire Safety in the Home*, a woman asked the officer representing the Fire Department where spot-type heat detectors should be placed in a room to give an alarm properly if fire should occur. The officer responded that the center of the ceiling was the best location. He added that any point on the ceiling was the next best, and, if it were necessary to mount the detector on a side wall, it should be placed at least 6 inches but no more than 12 inches from the ceiling. The officer's instructions to the citizen were
    A. *correct*
    B. *incorrect* in his statement of *any point on the ceiling*; spot-type detectors should not be placed on ceilings in the corner of rooms
    C. *incorrect* in his statement *at least 6 inches from the ceiling*
    D. *incorrect*; side wall locations for spot-type detectors are preferable to ceiling locations

22. Safety cans for indoor handling of small quantities of flammable liquids are approved when equipped with pouring outlets that have tight-fitting caps or valves which are normally kept closed by springs, except when manual pressure is applied to keep them open. During apparatus field inspection, a company officer finds that small unsafe containers are being utilized at a certain location. Wishing to use this discovery to convince the occupants of the premises of the superiority of the authorized container, the officer decides to explain the advantages of the approved type.
Of the following, the MOST complete and accurate explanation he could give is that the approved container
    A. prevents spillage if accidentally tipped over
    B. is self-venting if exposed to fire and prevents spillage if accidentally tipped over
    C. provides relief venting in case of explosion, is self-venting if exposed to fire, and prevents spillage if accidentally tipped over
    D. prevents a static charge from building up during pouring operations, provides relief venting in case of explosion, is self-venting if exposed to fire, and prevents spillage if accidentally tipped over

23. While inspecting a cylindrical gravity tank for an automatic sprinkler system, a chief observes that the water in the tank is 10 feet deep and that the tank has a diameter of 9 feet. He asks the building manager how many gallons are in the tank and receives the reply, *About 10,000.*

Based on his own observation and calculations, the chief should
- A. *agree* that the manager's answer is probably correct
- B. *disagree* with the manager's answer; the answer is more nearly 20,000 gallons
- C. *disagree* with the manager's answer; the answer is more nearly 15,000 gallons
- D. *disagree* with the manager's answer; the answer is more nearly 5,000 gallons

24. The one of the following that is NOT an accurate statement with respect to the findings of a survey conducted by a member of the National Commission on Fire Prevention and Control concerning the public's knowledge of fire safety is that
    - A. many youngsters indicated that they were likely to do something dangerous if a frying pan caught fire
    - B. many adults and most youngsters did not know that a 15-ampere fuse is the safest for ordinary household lighting circuits
    - C. most youngsters and adults indicated they would make the mistake of opening a hot door
    - D. most youngsters and adults did not know that carbon monoxide can rob them of their judgment and coordination

24.___

25. You are inspecting a building for violations. You must perform the following steps in the order given:
    - I. Find the manager of the building and introduce yourself.
    - II. Have the manager accompany you during the inspection.
    - III. Start the inspection by checking the Fire Department permits which have been issued to the building. The permits are located in the office of the building.
    - IV. Inspect the building for violations of the Fire Prevention Laws. Begin at the roof and work down to the basement or cellar.
    - V. As you inspect, write on a piece of paper any violations you find and explain them to the building manager.

    You are inspecting a supermarket. After entering the building, you identify yourself to the store manager and ask him to come along during the inspection.
    Which one of the following actions should you take NEXT?
    - A. Start inspecting the supermarket, beginning at the basement.
    - B. Start inspecting the supermarket, beginning at the roof.
    - C. Ask to see the Fire Department permits which have been issued to the supermarket.
    - D. Write down any violations which are seen while introducing yourself to the manager.

25.___

26. Many fires are caused by improper use of oxyacetylene torches.
    The MAIN cause of such fires is the
       A. high pressure under which the gases are stored
       B. failure to control or extinguish sparks
       C. high temperatures generated by the equipment
       D. explosive nature of the gases used

Questions 27-29.

DIRECTIONS: Questions 27 through 29 are to be answered on the basis of the following paragraph.

   The only openings permitted in fire partitions except openings for ventilating ducts shall be those required for doors. There shall be but one such door opening unless the provision of additional openings would not exceed in total width of all doorways 25 percent of the length of the wall. The minimum distance between openings shall be three feet. The maximum area for such a door opening shall be 80 square feet, except that such openings for the passage of motor trucks may be a maximum of 140 square feet.

27. According to the above paragraph, openings in fire partitions are permitted only for
       A. doors
       B. doors and windows
       C. doors and ventilation ducts
       D. doors, windows, and ventilation ducts

28. In a fire partition 22 feet long and 10 feet high, the MAXIMUM number of doors 3 feet wide and 7 feet high is
       A. 1   B. 2   C. 3   D. 4

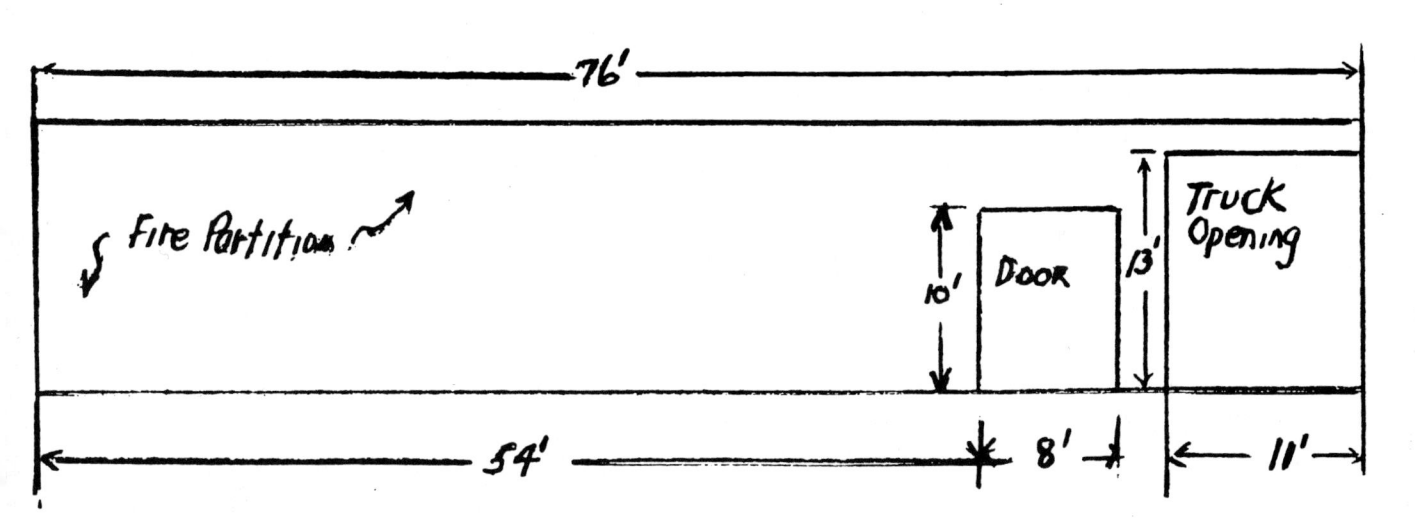

29.

The one of the following statements about the layout shown
on the preceding page that is MOST accurate is that the
  A. total width of the openings is too large
  B. truck opening is too large
  C. truck and door openings are too close together
  D. layout is acceptable

30. The Rules of the Board of Standards and Appeals provide   30.____
    that in a coin-operated dry-cleaning establishment
    spotting and sponging may be done by
     A. the general public or a qualified operator if water
        only is used
     B. a qualified operator if water only is used
     C. the general public if water only is used or by a
        qualified operator if inflammable liquids are used
     D. neither the general public nor a qualified operator

KEY (CORRECT ANSWERS)

1. B	11. B	21. B
2. B	12. C	22. B
3. C	13. B	23. D
4. B	14. D	24. C
5. B	15. A	25. C
6. A	16. D	26. B
7. D	17. D	27. C
8. A	18. D	28. A
9. D	19. C	29. B
10. C	20. A	30. B

TEST 4

DIRECTIONS: Each question or incomplete statement is followed by several suggested answers or completions. Select the one that BEST answers the question or completes the statement. *PRINT THE LETTER OF THE CORRECT ANSWER IN THE SPACE AT THE RIGHT.*

1. An officer is performing a routine quarterly inspection in a large motion picture theatre.
   Which one of the following actions taken by the officer during his inspection would generally be CORRECT?
   A. His first action is to proceed to the box office to review the theatre inspection log book.
   B. He informs the theatre owner that daily entries made by the owner in the log book should contain the name of the person designated to prevent any undue excitement or possible panic and indicate the location of the nearest street fire alarm box.
   C. Upon finding that the theatre owner has failed to maintain the log in the prescribed manner, the officer serves him with a summons.
   D. He examines the entries made since the previous inspection by an officer and records the results of this examination.

1.___

2. The owner of a building which comes under the jurisdiction of the Housing Maintenance Code would be in compliance with the Code if he
   A. installs, in a dwelling unit, a gas-fired refrigerator which is equipped with a flue assembly composed of non-metallic material
   B. obtains combustion air for the gas-fueled water heater in a bedroom in his new law tenement directly from the outer air
   C. connects each gas-fueled heater to the rigid gas piping supply line by means of a metallic flexible gas connection
   D. arranges to have the gas appliance in his old law tenement inspected by a licensed plumber on a biennial basis

2.___

3. Of the following activities, the one the code specifically permits bulk or waste oil recovery plants to do is
   A. refine waste oil for resale without a permit
   B. mix waste oil with No. 6 fuel oil for use in approved fuel oil burners
   C. transport waste oil in the vendor's container in 220 gallon quantities without a permit
   D. store waste oil in premises other than storage plants or buried tank systems in quantities greater than those restricting other combustible oils

3.___

4. A chief, visiting a company performing apparatus field inspection, is informed by the lieutenant in command of a hazardous situation just encountered in a fur processing plant. In the presence of the factory manager, the two officers discussed various sections of the Administrative Code which might be relevant and several approaches to the problem that could be taken by the fire department to abate the hazard. Finally, the chief directed the lieutenant to issue certain orders to the manager. Discussing this problem in the presence of the manager was
   A. *proper*, mainly because he probably would realize that the fire department was not acting arbitrarily or unreasonably
   B. *improper*, mainly because he might prefer one of the approaches which was suggested and rejected
   C. *proper*, mainly because the activities of the fire department should, whenever possible, be open to the public
   D. *improper*, mainly because inaccurate statements may have been made during the preliminary discussion

5. A chief supervising apparatus field inspection duty activities comes upon a company just as it is completing inspection of a clothing manufacturing plant. The lieutenant in command reports that the company has issued minor violation orders for five conditions which they discovered. The chief considers four of the conditions cited clear violations of the Administrative Code. The fifth condition he considers a borderline case which he, himself, would not have handled by issuing a violation order.
   In this situation, the BEST of the following courses for the chief to take is to
   A. direct the lieutenant to cancel the violation order for the borderline situation
   B. say nothing to the lieutenant at this time but later warn him against unduly strict interpretation of the Administrative Code
   C. accept the lieutenant's findings without any comment at this time or later
   D. question the lieutenant closely about various sections of the Administrative Code to determine whether he has a proper understanding of its requirements

Questions 6-7.

DIRECTIONS: Questions 6 and 7 are to be answered SOLELY on the basis of the following passage.

Following is a list of rules for fire extinguishers which are required in different types of public buildings in the city:

Rule 1: Hospitals, nursing homes, hotels, and motels must have one $2\frac{1}{2}$ gallon water extinguisher for every 2,500 square feet, or part thereof, of floor area on each floor.

Rule 2: Stores with floor areas of 1,500 square feet or less must have one 2½ gallon water extinguisher. Stores with floor areas of over 1,500 square feet must have one 2½ gallon water extinguisher for every 2,500 square feet, or part thereof, of floor area on each floor.

Rule 3: Kitchens must have one 2½ gallon foam extinguisher or one 5 pound dry chemical extinguisher for every 1,250 square feet, or part thereof, of floor area on each floor. For kitchen areas, this rule is in addition to Rules 1 and 2.

6. An inspector is inspecting a one-story nursing home which has a total of 3,000 square feet of floor area. This includes a kitchen, which is 1,500 square feet in area, in the rear of the floor.
Of the following, the inspector should conclude that the nursing home should be equipped with _____ extinguisher(s) and _____ extinguisher(s).
   A. 1 water; 1 foam   B. 1 water; 1 dry chemical
   C. 2 water; 2 foam   D. 2 foam; 1 dry chemical

7. An inspector is inspecting a store which has two floors. The first floor has 2,600 square feet. The second floor has 1,450 square feet.
The store should be equipped with AT LEAST
   A. two 2½ gallon water extinguishers, one for each floor
   B. three 2½ gallon water extinguishers, two for the first floor and one for the second floor
   C. two 2½ gallon foam extinguishers, one for each floor
   D. two 2½ gallon extinguishers, either foam or water, one for each floor

8. A recycling sprinkler head called *The Aquamatic* has been developed that will turn itself off after the fire is extinguished and turn itself on again if the fire should rekindle.
Of the following, it would generally be INACCURATE to state that this recycling sprinkler head
   A. has been approved by the Underwriters' Laboratories for installation where there is high risk of flash fires
   B. is capable of discharging 30 gpm and is approved by the Underwriters' Laboratories for use in systems engineered to make maximum use of available water
   C. eliminates the need to turn off the main valve to replace Aquamatic elements
   D. has a 165° temperature rating, the usual ½ inch national pipe thread, is mounted in the pendant position and is approved for installation in any sprinkler system, new or old

9. Assume that you are supervising a scheduled inspection of auxiliary fire protection equipment in a tunnel in the absence of a deputy chief.
   In supervising the inspection, it would be appropriate for you to do all of the following EXCEPT
   A. utilize the members of the Rescue Company in carrying out specific inspectional duties
   B. notify the dispatcher of the units participating, the designated radio contact, and the units which are not available for response to their assigned alarms
   C. make a written recommendation suggesting a corrective procedure to upgrade a particular piece of inadequate equipment
   D. forward referrals and recommendations through official channels to the division of fire prevention for transmittal to the various agencies concerned and for necessary follow-up

10. What was formerly known as the *spray sprinkler* is now designated as the *standard sprinkler* and is generally similar in appearance to the old type head.
    Of the following, the MOST NEARLY accurate statement about the modern one-half inch sprinkler head is that
    A. a larger area of coverage is secured by directing all the water downward and horizontally
    B. the present upright spray sprinkler operates on the direct spray principle
    C. major changes in deflector design have reduced discharge capacities, but have increased particle division
    D. there is increased exposure to the ceiling, but more direct discharge on the burning materials

11. The one of the following which is generally a CORRECT statement about automatic deluge sprinkler systems is that they are
    A. installed in properties when there is a danger of serious water damage due to accidental functioning
    B. equipped with quartzoid bulb type activators in lieu of fusible links
    C. controlled by a quick-opening valve known as the deluge valve
    D. ineffective where ceilings are unusually high and heads would not open quickly enough

12. An inspection of the private class 3 box cards of the computerized alarm assignment system should reveal that the cards PROPERLY list the
    A. company numbers of those engine and ladder companies responding to each terminal under the *Response Policy* column
    B. battalion number of the battalion chief assigned to respond to each terminal under the *B.C.* column
    C. company numbers of the engine and ladder companies assigned to the associated street box
    D. address of the alarm service company

13. The General Accounting Office in Washington publicized the fact that there is a possible defect in some models of a certain smoke detector.
    The one of the following which BEST describes this defect is that these detectors
    A. failed to signal an alarm under heavy smoke conditions
    B. expected battery life is only three months or less
    C. have smoke entry vents which are too narrow so that dust tends to render the detectors ineffective
    D. are overheating and, in time, tend to self-ignite

14. Assume that you are a fire officer who has been asked to address a local community group on the relative merits of smoke and heat detectors and the proper placement, operation, and maintenance of the various types of detectors. During this meeting, it would be MOST appropriate for you to point out that
    A. it is more advisable to install a smoke detector than a heat detector in the kitchen
    B. placement of a smoke detector in a room below an insulated attic should be on the ceiling towards the center of the room
    C. placing a smoke detector in the hallway near each sleeping area and on every floor level not containing a sleeping area will provide minimal protection
    D. a smoke detector installed on the ceiling near a doorway should be placed closer to the wall above the doorway than the distance from the ceiling to the top of the door

15. The basic multiple-death fire safety problem in nursing home facilities is GENERALLY considered to be the failure to
    A. confine the fire's resultant products of combustion to the room of origin
    B. conduct and properly supervise comprehensive fire exit and evacuation drills
    C. adequately service and maintain existing smoke-detection and smoke-control systems
    D. reduce the combustible contents of patients' rooms and enforcement of the no-smoking restrictions by a trained staff

16. The basic assumption of fire prevention educational programs is that people frequently
    A. must be forced into obeying fire laws
    B. are unaware of the dangers involved in some of their actions
    C. don't care whether or not their actions are dangerous
    D. assume that fire insurance protects them against all fire loss

Questions 17-19.

DIRECTIONS: Questions 17 through 19 are to be answered on the basis of the following paragraph.

Unlined linen hose is essentially a fabric tube made of closely woven linen yarn. Due to the natural characteristics of linen, very shortly after water is introduced, the threads swell after being wet, closing the minute spaces between them making the tube practically water-tight. This type of hose tends to deteriorate rapidly if not thoroughly dried after use or if installed where it will be exposed to dampness or the weather. It is not ordinarily built to withstand frequent service or for use where the fabric will be subjected to chafing from rough or sharp surfaces.

17. Seepage of water through an unlined linen hose is observed when the water is first turned on.
    From the above paragraph, we may conclude that the seepage
    A. indicates that the hose is defective
    B. does not indicate that the hose is defective provided that the seepage is proportionate to the water pressure
    C. does not indicate that the hose is defective provided that the seepage is greatly reduced when the hose becomes thoroughly wet
    D. does not indicate that the hose is defective provided that the seepage takes place only at the surface of the hose

18. Unlined linen hose is MOST suitable for use
    A. as a garden hose
    B. on fire department apparatus
    C. as emergency fire equipment in buildings
    D. in fire department training schools

19. The use of unlined linen hose would be LEAST appropriate in a(n)
    A. outdoor lumber yard
    B. non-fireproof office building
    C. department store
    D. cosmetic manufacturing plant

20. Doors in theatres and other places of public assembly usually open outwardly.
    The MAIN reason for this requirement is, in the event of fire, to
    A. provide the widest possible passageway for escape of the audience
    B. prevent panic-stricken audience from jamming the doors in a closed position
    C. indicate to the audience the safe direction of travel
    D. prevent unauthorized persons from entering the building

21. Fire prevention inspections should be conducted at irregular hours or intervals.
    The BEST justification for this *irregularity* is that it permits the firemen to
    A. make inspections when they have free time
    B. see the inspected establishments in their normal condition and not in their *dressed-up* condition
    C. avoid making inspections at times which would be inconvenient for the inspected establishments
    D. concentrate their inspectional activities on those establishments which present the greatest fire hazard

22. Static electricity is a hazard in industry CHIEFLY because it may cause
    A. dangerous or painful burns
    B. chemical decomposition of toxic elements
    C. sparks which can start an explosion
    D. overheating of electrical equipment

Questions 23-25.

DIRECTIONS: Questions 23 through 25 are to be answered on the basis of the following paragraph.

A plastic does not consist of a single substance, but is a blended combination of several. In addition to the resin, it may contain various fillers, plasticizers, lubricants, and coloring material. Depending upon the type and quantity of substances added to the binder, the properties, including combustibility, may be altered considerably. The flammability of plastics depends upon the composition and, as with other materials, upon their physical size and condition. Thin sections, sharp edges, or powdered plastics will ignite and burn more readily than the same amount of identical material in heavy sections with smooth surfaces.

23. According to the above paragraph, all plastics contain a
    A. resin
    B. resin and a filler
    C. resin, filler, and plasticizer
    D. resin, filler, plasticizer, lubricant, and coloring material

24. The one of the following conclusions that is BEST supported by the above paragraph is that the flammability of plastics
    A. generally is high   B. generally is moderate
    C. generally is low   D. varies considerably

25. According to the above paragraph, *plastics* can BEST be described as
    A. a trade name
    B. the name of a specific product
    C. the name of a group of products which have some similar and some dissimilar properties
    D. the name of any substance which can be shaped or molded during the production process

26. While on inspection duty, an inspector discovers the superintendent of a tenement just starting to remove boxes and other material which are blocking hallways. Apparently, the superintendent started removal as soon as he saw the inspector approach.
In this situation, it is MOST important that the inspector
   A. warn the superintendent of the penalties for violation of the Fire Prevention Code
   B. help the superintendent remove the material blocking the hallways
   C. commend the superintendent for his efforts to maintain a safe building
   D. check again, after completing the inspection, to see whether the material has been removed completely

27. Persons engaged in certain hazardous activities are required to obtain a Fire Department permit or certificate for which a fee is charged.
The MAIN reason for requiring permits or certificates is to
   A. obtain revenue for the city government
   B. prevent unqualified persons from engaging in these activities
   C. obtain information about these activities in order to plan for fire emergencies
   D. warn the public of the hazardous nature of these activities

28. An inspector, on his way to work, is stopped by a citizen who complains that the employees of a nearby store frequently pile empty crates and boxes in a doorway, blocking passage.
The one of the following which would be the MOST appropriate action for the inspector to take is to
   A. assure the citizen that the fire department's inspectional activities will eventually *catch up* with the store
   B. obtain the address of the store and investigate to determine whether the citizen's complaint is justified
   C. obtain the address of the store and report the complaint to his superior officer
   D. ask the citizen for specific dates on which this practice has occurred to determine whether the complaint is justified

29. While inspecting a business building, you discover an oil burner installation with the following features:
   I. Installed on the third story, whose floor is 40' above the street level
   II. Oil delivery lines to the burner are one and one-half inches iron pipe size, and
   III. Pressure in the oil lines to the burner is 25 lbs. per square inch

The one of the following statements concerning this installation and the applicable sections of the rules of the Board of Standards and Appeals that is MOST accurate is that
A. feature I is a violation of the rules
B. feature II is a violation of the rules
C. feature III is a violation of the rules
D. the installation complies with the rules

30. The Fire Department now uses companies on fire duty, with their apparatus, for fire prevention inspection in commercial buildings.
The one of the following changes which was MOST important in making this inspection procedure practicable was the
A. reduction of hours of work of firemen
B. use of two-way radio equipment
C. use of enclosed cabs on fire apparatus
D. increase in property values during the post-war period

KEY (CORRECT ANSWERS)

1. C	11. D	21. B
2. D	12. B	22. C
3. D	13. B	23. A
4. D	14. B	24. D
5. C	15. A	25. C
6. C	16. B	26. D
7. B	17. C	27. B
8. C	18. C	28. C
9. D	19. A	29. D
10. A	20. B	30. B

EXAMINATION SECTION
TEST 1

Directions: Each question or incomplete statement is followed by several suggested answers or completions. Select the one the BEST answers the question or completes the statement. *PRINT THE LETTER OF THE CORRECT ANSWER IN THE SPACE AT THE RIGHT.*

1) The pivotal factor in determining whether an event is an "emergency" is typically

A. the degree to which the event was unexpected
B. whether the event requires supplemental efforts to save lives and protect property, public health and safety
C. whether the event causes a loss of life
D. the severity and magnitude of the damage caused by the event

1.____

2) Which of the following is an activity that is included within the authority of the Federal Emergency Management Agency (FEMA)?

A. Physically rescuing disaster victims
B. Establishing building standards and zoning regulations that will help mitigate the adverse effects of a disaster
C. Providing mobile communications systems that open emergency lines when commercial networks are down
D. Taking the lead role in recovery efforts after a disaster

2.____

3) Which of the following is NOT a member of the command staff under the incident command system?

A. Information officer
B. Information officer
C. Logistics officer
D. Safety officer

3.____

4) The Federal Response Plan generally performs each of the following functions, EXCEPT

A. grouping types of federal assistance under twelve emergency support functions
B. designating a primary agency and support agency for each emergency support function
C. providing loans and grants to state and local governments
D. explaining how the federal government mobilizes and supports state and local response efforts

4.____

5) Under the Federal Response Plan, FEMA is the lead agency for the   5. _____
emergency support functions (ESFs) of

    I.   Resources Support
    II.   Communications
    III.   Information and Planning
    IV.   Urban Search and Rescue

A.   I only
B.   II and III
C.   III and IV
D.   I, II, III and IV

Questions 6 through 10 refer to the following scenario:

A freak winter storm has stalled out over Summit County, dropping a record 25 inches of snow in a single night. More snow is forecast over the next 2 days, and the temperature is supposed to remain well below freezing for at least the next week or so.

All over the county, stranded motorists and residents without power have overwhelmed the 911 dispatch center. Although road crews have been activated, many of the drivers can't get to their trucks. Local and state emergency operations centers have been activated, and a local state of emergency has been declared. The incident commander has set up the command post at the police precinct house in the heart of the downtown in the county seat. The incident will require a large number and range of resources.

6) The incident commander will activate general staff positions that will   6. _____
each be led by a(n)

A.   branch supervisor
B.   staging area manager
C.   division supervisor
D.   section chief

7) Because this incident covers a large geographic area and is likely to   7. _____
continue for a period of time, the incident commander should probably establish a(n)

A.   base
B.   casualty collection point
C.   staging area
D.   camp

8) After several hours, the operations section activates several staging areas, divisions, branches, and groups. Under the ICS's principle of unity of command, which of these managers are likely to report directly to the incident commander?

A. only the operations section chief
B. the operations section chief and the staging area managers
C. branch supervisors and division leaders
D. any of the above managers

8. _____

9) The incident commander has requested that the state department of transportation send road-clearing equipment to help with the incident. The department's representative would communicate with the incident command staff's

A. information officer
B. planning section chief
C. liaison officer
D. facilities unit manager

9. _____

10) After several days, a worker at the ICP is told that his position will be demobilized at the conclusion of the current operational period. The worker should

    I. update all files and records
    II. complete all work in progress, unless otherwise directed
    III. return or otherwise transfer custody of all equipment that he has signed for
    IV. brief his relief or immediate supervisor on the status of all work, pending assignments, needs, and special situations

A. I and II
B. II only
C. II, III and IV
D. I, II, III and IV

10. _____

11) As defined by disaster relief agencies, weapons of mass destruction (WMDs) include

    I. radiation or radioactivity
    II. diseases or organisms
    III. toxic or poisonous chemicals, or their precursors

A. I only
B. I and II
C. II and III
D. I, II and III

11. _____

12) Without a presidential declaration of disaster, federal disaster assistance may include each of the following, EXCEPT   12. _____

A. firefighting assistance
B. tax refunds
C. unemployment insurance
D. search and rescue

13) Typically, hazard analysis determines   13. _____

   I. how hazards are likely to affect the community
   II. when the next disaster is most likely to occur
   III. how well the community will be able to respond to a disaster
   IV. the costs of risk

A. I only
B. I and II
C. I, III and IV
D. I, II, III and IV

14) Each of the following is a responsibility of an incident commander, EXCEPT   14. _____

A. managing assigned resources
B. maintaining accountability
C. coordinating the community-wide response
D. protecting life and property

15) Federal mission assignments   15. _____

A. may be requested by counties and cities
B. are usually issued to meet all eligible requests for federal assistance
C. can be issued before a disaster declaration
D. meet needs that exceed state and local government resources

16) The federal government's most important contribution to hazard mitigation efforts in any given community will likely be to   16. _____

A. ensure that all federal facilities in the community are built or retrofitted to reduce hazard vulnerability
B. provide adequate funding for hazard mitigation
C. take a leadership role in the planning stages of hazard mitigation activities
D. controlling the costs of over-ambitious state and local mitigation programs

17) "Unity of command" in the incident command system refers to the fact that   17. _____

A. each member reports to only one supervisor
B. each member reports to the incident commander
C. all members share responsibility for decision-making in the operations function of incident response
D. all members share responsibility for overall incident management

18) An emergency operations plan (EOP)   18. _____

    I. assigns responsibility for mitigation concerns to local officials
    II. explains how people and property will be protected in emergencies
    III. identifies resources available for use during response and recovery operations
    IV. establishes lines of authority

A. I and II
B. II and III
C. II, III and IV
D. III and IV

19) What component of emergency management is defined as "sustained actions taken to reduce or eliminate the long-term risk to people and property from hazards and their effects?"   19. _____

A. Risk analysis
B. Vulnerability assessment
C. Preparedness
D. Mitigation

20) Under federal regulations, all organizations that respond to _____ incidents are required to use the incident command system.   20. _____

    I. flood
    II. fire
    III. hazardous materials
    IV. hurricane or tornado

A. I only
B. I, II and IV
C. II and III
D. III only

21) Which of the following is a federal program that funds state and local pre-disaster floodplain planning and projects?

A. Flood Mitigation Assistance
B. 406
C. Increased Cost of Compliance
D. Hazard Mitigation Grant

22) The Community Rating System is an element of the National Flood Insurance Program that can

    I. decrease a community's flood insurance premiums
    II. provide an incentive for new flood mitigation, planning, and preparedness activities
    III. increase a community's flood insurance premiums
    IV. be made available to non-NFIP communities

A. I only
B. I and II
C. I and III
D. I, II, III and IV

23) At the scene of a major storm, an operations section chief understands that her span of control will be exceeded when the requested resources arrive. There is a need to assign resources geographically. One effective way to maintain her span of control would be to assign personnel to

A. units
B. divisions
C. bases
D. strike teams

24) The federal emergency public assistance program provides funds to

A. businesses for economic recovery after a disaster
B. individuals for temporary housing
C. private nonprofit universities and colleges for mitigation research
D. state and local governments for response and recovery activities

25) The federal cost share for _____ programs is 100%

A. emergency work
B. crisis counseling
C. permanent, restorative work
D. "other needs" assistance

KEY (CORRECT ANSWERS)

1. B
2. C
3. C
4. C
5. C

6. D
7. A
8. A
9. C
10. D

11. D
12. C
13. A
14. C
15. D

16. A
17. A
18. C
19. D
20. D

21. A
22. B
23. B
24. D
25. B

TEST 2

Directions: Each question or incomplete statement is followed by several suggested answers or completions. Select the one the BEST answers the question or completes the statement. *PRINT THE LETTER OF THE CORRECT ANSWER IN THE SPACE AT THE RIGHT.*

1) An effective emergency management plan is characterized by

    I. overlapping command functions between jurisdictions
    II. modular organization
    III. separate police and fire command posts
    IV. common terminology

A. I only
B. I and III
C. II and IV
D. I, II, III and IV

1. _____

2) Emergency Management Mutual Aid (EMMA) is

    I. a means of establishing federal control over a disaster situation
    II. coordinated by FEMA
    III. a system for moving emergency management personnel to other jurisdictions that need assistance
    IV. a way of providing continuous 24-hour-a-day management during a disaster

A. I only
B. I and II
C. III and IV
D. I, II, III and IV

2. _____

3) A combination of personnel and equipment—such as a search and rescue team and an EMS team assigned to locate and treat several people trapped in the debris of a building collapse—is usually called a(n) _____ in the incident command system.

A. division
B. task force
C. unit
D. strike team

3. _____

4) In the Federal Response Plan, an Emergency Support Team (EST)   4. _____

A. responds to presidential disaster or emergency declarations
B. coordinates multi-state and multi-regional operations
C. deploys to high-visibility, catastrophic disasters
D. coordinates early response operations with the state

5) Disaster loans for homeowners, renters, business owners and nonprofit organizations are administered and funded by the   5. _____

A. Small Business Administration (SBA)
B. Department of Housing and Urban Development (HUD)
C. Federal Emergency Management Agency (FEMA)
D. American Red Cross

Questions 6 through 9 refer to the following scenario:

At around midnight, the 911 call center receives a call from the maintenance department of a local nursing home. Fire alarms have sounded in the west residential hall, which is a four-story wing. Smoke can be seen from the fourth floor. The hall houses 300 residents, and there are reports that some residents are trapped inside.

Fire Battalion 6 is immediately dispatched. After an initial assessment, the Battalion Chief requests a general alarm and assigns a safety officer, a liaison officer, and a full general staff.

6) The first priority of the planning section will be to   6. _____

A. develop response goals and objectives
B. monitor safety conditions
C. assess the resource needs of the situation
D. contact other agencies assigned to the incident

7) In addition to the incident command post, the incident will require   7. _____

  I. at least one staging area
  II. several bases
  III. a casualty collection point (CCP)
  IV. a camp

A. I only
B. I and III
C. II, III and IV
D. I, II, III and IV

8) A local counselor, a trauma expert, is asked to help calm arriving family members who fear their loved ones are trapped in the fire. Upon arriving at the scene, the counselor should check in with the _____ unit of the planning section.

8. _____

A. medical
B. ground support
C. facilities
D. resources

9) Search and rescue teams are able to locate most, but not all, of the victims from the building. After some time, it becomes clear that these victims are dead. The incident commander has requested that several local churches, synagogues, and mosques help provide short-term shelter for the newly homeless victims of the fire. He has also requested the help of several local mental health professionals to assist the family members who are grieving for the dead. After representatives from these outside agencies check in, they should work with the

9. _____

A. liaison officer
B. planning section chief
C. logistics section chief
D. safety officer

10) Which of the following is an activity that is NOT included within the authority of the Federal Emergency Management Agency (FEMA)?

10. _____

A. Administering the National Flood Insurance Program
B. Providing "buy out" funding to relocate homes and businesses away from high-risk areas
C. Creating risk assessment maps to aid local planners
D. Operating temporary feeding stations or shelters after a disaster

11) Under the incident command system, which of the following has the authority to bypass the chain of command when necessary?

11. _____

A. Logistics officer
B. Liaison officer
C. Operations section chief
D. Safety officer

12) Which of the following agencies provides AmeriCorps assistance following a disaster?

12. _____

A. Peace Corps
B. Corporation for National Service (CNS)
C. Department of Labor
D. Department of Health and Human Services

13) A community that wants to participate in the National Flood Insurance   13. _____
Program must

    I.   elevate roadbeds and homes that lie within a floodplain
    II.   eliminate all known flood hazards
    III.   adopt and enforce a floodplain management ordinance
    IV.   conduct a flood hazard assessment

A.   I only
B.   II only
C.   III only
D.   III and IV

14) In federal mission assignment processing, which of the following   14. _____
typically occurs FIRST?

A.   the mission assignment is routed in the National Emergency Management Information System (NEMIS) for electronic signature
B.   the mission assignment coordinator or action tracker enters information from the action request form into the National Emergency Management Information System (NEMIS)
C.   funds are obligated in the financial system for mission assignment
D.   an operations section chief directs issuance of a mission assignment

15) Upon arrival at the scene of a disaster, the response team's FIRST   15. _____
action would most likely be to

A.   form initial opinions about the incident's requirements
B.   appoint a logistics officer
C.   develop an action plan
D.   establish a media liaison

16) The predicted impact that a hazard would have on people, services,   16. _____
facilities, and structures in a community is known specifically as

A.   vulnerability
B.   hazard identification
C.   risk
D.   incidence

17) A state that is considered a "Managing State" under FEMA's mitigation programs

    I. contributes up to 80 percent of HMGP project costs
    II. has concluded a Memorandum of Understanding (MOU) with FEMA to perform specific Hazard Mitigation Grant Program project review functions
    III. reviews infrastructure projects for mitigation opportunities
    IV. can approve Hazard Mitigation Grant Program projects subject to environmental review.

A. I and III
B. II and IV
C. II, III and IV
D. I, II, III and IV

17. _____

18) Which of the following is NOT a member of the general staff of an incident command system?

A. Logistics officer
B. Operations section chief
C. Safety officer
D. Incident commander

18. _____

19) The lists of hazards developed during a hazard analysis will be compiled using

    I. community records
    II. historical data
    III. existing hazard analyses
    IV. computer simulations

A. I and II
B. I, II, and III
C. III only
D. I, II, III and IV

19. _____

20) Which of the following is NEVER an allowable cost that can be submitted by states to federal disaster reimbursement programs?

A. advertisements seeking temporary personnel for the disaster recovery efforts
B. services of state building inspectors
C. expenses incurred by the Officer of the Governor
D. messenger/courier services

20. _____

21) The STAPLE criteria are a means of determining the feasibility of _____ actions.

A. mitigation
B. preparation
C. response
D. recovery

21. _____

22) An incident command system has been fully expanded to accommodate large-scale operations. In this case, the staging area manager would report to the

A. operations section chief
B. incident commander
C. facilities unit leader
D. logistics officer

22. _____

23) At the state level, which of the following actions would occur at the "response" phase of disaster response?

A. issuing a disaster proclamation
B. requesting federal assistance
C. conducting mitigation efforts
D. activating and staffing an emergency operations center

23. _____

24) The responsibility for identifying hazards and launching mitigation strategies typically belongs to

A. the federal government
B. state governments
C. local governments
D. businesses and individuals

24. _____

25) FEMA's role in disaster assistance includes

I. responding to requests from local governments
II. managing the president's Disaster Relief Fund
III. evaluating a state's request for a presidential declaration
IV. advising the president on whether or not to make a declaration

A. I and II
B. III only
C. II, III and IV
D. I, II, III and IV

25. _____

KEY (CORRECT ANSWERS)

1. C
2. C
3. B
4. B
5. A

6. C
7. B
8. D
9. A
10. D

11. D
12. B
13. C
14. D
15. A

16. C
17. B
18. D
19. B
20. C

21. A
22. A
23. B
24. C
25. C

EXAMINATION SECTION
TEST 1

Directions: Each question or incomplete statement is followed by several suggested answers or completions. Select the one the BEST answers the question or completes the statement. *PRINT THE LETTER OF THE CORRECT ANSWER IN THE SPACE AT THE RIGHT.*

1) Typically, the primary responsibility for mitigation lies at the level of the

A. state government
B. individual citizens in a community
C. federal government
D. local government

1. _____

2) Loss protection systems include

 I. land use restrictions
 II. seismic retrofitting
 III. evacuation plans
 IV. early-alert systems

A. I and IV
B. I, II and III
C. I and III
D. I, II, III and IV

2. _____

3) At the scene of any emergency, the first priority of the incident commander is

A. assessing incident priorities
B. life safety
C. stabilizing the incident
D. coordinating overall emergency activities

3. _____

4) Which of the authorities belongs exclusively to the federal government when an incident occurs?

A. Coordinating federal, state, local and volunteer agencies
B. Developing an Emergency Operations Plan
C. Evacuating citizens
D. Conducting preliminary damage assessments

4. _____

5) Of the following, which type of federal assistance is provided EARLIEST during the emergency response process?

A. SBA loans
B. Insurance
C. Cora Brown Fund
D. Housing assistance

Questions 6 through 9 refer to the following scenario:

At a large resort hotel in a popular tourist port, a member of the kitchen staff spills a five-gallon bucket of caustic cleaner onto a hot griddle. The fumes immediately fill the kitchen, which is immediately evacuated, and enter the hotel's ventilation system. Within an hour, the hotel's front desk is receiving calls complaining of severe respiratory problems, nausea, vomiting, and severely irritated eyes, noses, and mouths. The hotel manager called the local 911 center immediately after the first call, and an ambulance and EMS team were sent to the scene. As many more guests reported their symptoms, additional medical teams were sent and the local hospital's emergency room was put on notice. Within two hours of the spill, more than 90 guests had requested help. More than 300 people are currently staying in the hotel.

Local resources are exhausted by the first two hours' emergency calls, and additional victims must be transported to other hospitals, some of which are more than 75 miles from the hotel. Helicopters will be needed for transport.

6) The incident commander will need to establish

I. two bases
II. at least one more incident command post
III. a helibase
IV. at least one staging area

A. I and III
B. II, III and IV
C. III and IV
D. I, II, III and IV

7) The incident command system is fully expanded within the first three hours. The base manager will report to the

A. planning section chief
B. operations section chief
C. situation unit leader
D. facilities unit leader

8) The incident commander receives hourly updates from the operations section chief on the status of resources. Resources at an incident will always be characterized as

A. committed, unavailable, or at rest
B. available or unavailable
C. assigned, en route, or unavailable
D. available, assigned, or out-of-service

8. _____

9) After the first few calls to the 911 center, the media are reporting rumors of a possible terror attack on the hotel. The incident commander should immediately establish a(n)

A. communications center
B. liaison officer
C. press conference
D. information officer

9. _____

10) Under the incident command system, which of the following is NOT a designated facility?

A. Incident command post
B. Casualty collection point
C. Staging area
D. Perimeter post

10. _____

11) In the federal emergency public assistance process, the specialist is responsible for

A. conducting applicants' briefings
B. designing large projects
C. coordinating with the state government
D. validating small projects

11. _____

12) The most common natural disasters in the United States are

A. earthquakes
B. wildland fires
C. tornadoes
D. floods

12. _____

13) Under the model of the incident command system, any function not assigned by the incident commander

A. becomes the charge of the liaison officer
B. is shared equally among battalion chiefs
C. is the responsibility of the incident commander
D. becomes the charge of the safety officer

14) At the state level, which of the following actions would occur at the "threat" or "impact" phase of disaster response?

A. evaluating the need for federal assistance
B. mobilizing resources
C. beginning infrastructure support
D. identifying staffing needs

15) The federal Hazard Mitigation Grant program offers federal assistance of up to _____% of the cost of eligible post-disaster state and local mitigation measures.

A. 25
B. 49
C. 75
D. 100

16) Under the incident command system, resources are kept at the _____ while awaiting incident assignments.

A. emergency operations center
B. cache
C. staging area
D. incident command post

17) To clear roadways of debris in the aftermath of a major storm, the incident commander requests four Type 2 bulldozers. In this case, the resources have been classified

A. by both type and kind
B. by type
C. by kind
D. as single resources

18) Under federal mission assignments assistance, direct federal assistance   18. _____

A. is usually 100 percent federally funded
B. supports federal responders
C. is subject to cost share
D. is requested by local governments

19) Of the following steps in preparing an "After-Action" report, which would be performed FIRST?   19. _____

A. Identifying unsolved problems
B. Selecting issues that are focal points
C. Developing recommendations on key issues for the main body of the report
D. Identifying problems that have policy implications

20) In emergency management, the determination of a disaster's probability and impact is known specifically as   20. _____

A. risk assessment
B. vulnerability analysis
C. risk management
D. risk analysis

21) Under the incident command system, a unit manager reports directly to the   21. _____

A. group supervisor
B. branch supervisor
C. logistics officer
D. section chief

22) In the financial management of a disaster, "allocation" refers to   22. _____

A. the request and receipt of payments into a grantee's account
B. setting aside funds for a specific program
C. any payment to liquidate an obligation
D. any formal reservation of funds

23) Which of the following is a structural solution to a flood hazard?   23. _____

A. Dam
B. Levee
C. Land use planning
D. Wet floodproofing

24) Under the incident command system, the organizational level that has responsibility for a specified functional assignment at an incident is managed by a

A. unit leader
B. group supervisor
C. section chief
D. branch director

24. _____

25) The main purpose of a Rapid Needs Assessment (RNA) at the state level is to

A. determine the resources necessary to conduct life-saving and life-sustaining operations during the emergency response phase of a disaster
B. provide voluntary agencies with information so they can assign the appropriate response staff
C. gather information to support the governor's request for a presidential disaster declaration
D. secure resources from unaffected areas of the state and disaster relief organizations

25. _____

KEY (CORRECT ANSWERS)

1. D
2. D
3. B
4. A
5. B

6. C
7. D
8. D
9. D
10. D

11. D
12. D
13. C
14. A
15. C

16. C
17. A
18. C
19. A
20. D

21. B
22. B
23. B
24. B
25. A

TEST 2

Directions: Each question or incomplete statement is followed by several suggested answers or completions. Select the one the BEST answers the question or completes the statement. *PRINT THE LETTER OF THE CORRECT ANSWER IN THE SPACE AT THE RIGHT.*

1) Which of the following is NOT associated with the response phase of emergency management?

1. _____

A. Debris removal
B. Access control
C. Mass care
D. Rebuilding structures

2) In the midst of a major storm, a city bus has gone over an embankment and overturned on the edge of a wooded area. The required triage and treatment would BEST be performed at a(n)

2. _____

A. base
B. staging area
C. casualty collection point
D. command and control point

3) In emergency management, the term "vulnerability analysis" is most accurately defined as

3. _____

A. the process of intervening to reduce risk
B. the determination of the likelihood of an event occurring and the consequences of its occurrence
C. a systematic method of determining the cost of risk
D. the determination of the possible hazards that may cause harm

4) Under the model of the incident command system, an incident commander is responsible for

4. _____

   I. evaluating plan effectiveness
   II. gathering and assigning resources
   III. communicating with other officials within the system
   IV. coordinating the overall incident response

A. I and II
B. II, III and IV
C. III only
D. I, II, III and IV

5) The mechanism by which FEMA provides funding to states to develop and maintain emergency management capabilities is the

5. _____

A. Performance Partnership Agreement (PPA)
B. National Mitigation Strategy
C. Emergency Management Mutual Aid (EMMA)
D. Community Rating System

Questions 6 through 9 refer to the following scenario:

At around 10:30 a.m. on a weekday afternoon, a receptionist at Glenwood Federal Bank receives a call from a person claiming to have planted a bomb in the area of the bank. Because the bank manager could not immediately be located, the receptionist called the local police department to report the call and ask for help. Three patrol cars and a bomb disposal unit arrived at the bank within minutes of the receptionist's call.

6) The initial incident commander for this incident would be the

6. _____

A. senior member of the bank staff
B. receptionist
C. senior member of the arriving police contingent
D. bank manager

7) Which of the following tasks should be performed FIRST by the incident commander at the bank?

7. _____

A. Cordoning off the bank
B. Setting up an information center
C. Establishing command
D. Evaluating the seriousness of the bomb threat

8) The incident commander should FIRST set up a(n)

8. _____

A. media center
B. incident command post (ICP)
C. casualty collection point (CCP)
D. staging area

9) After completing her initial assessment, the incident commander recognized a need for additional police officers. Under the incident command system, she would be requesting

A. a division
B. a task force
C. single resources
D. a strike force

9. _____

10) Primary logistical functions for an incident are coordinated and administered at a(n)

A. incident command post
B. staging area
C. base
D. mobilization center

10. _____

11) The president may deny a request for a disaster declaration if

I. the preliminary damage assessment is submitted on the incorrect forms
II. the federal government determines that other sources can provide adequate assistance
III. state and local governments are able to provide the necessary assistance
IV. the federal legislature overturns the declaration

A. I only
B. II and III
C. II and IV
D. I, II, III and IV

11. _____

12) A county's division of emergency management is seeking funds to retrofit its public buildings in order to make them more resistant to seismic activity. The county should apply for a _____ grant from the federal government

A. disaster aid
B. public assistance
C. temporary disaster housing
D. hazard mitigation

12. _____

24) At the state level, the Governor's Authorized Representative 24. ____

A. interfaces with the Federal Coordinating Officer (FCO)
B. executes all necessary documents on behalf of the State
C. establishes a Disaster Field Office (DFO) and Disaster Recovery Centers (DRC)
D. directs the activities of state departments and agencies

25) The incident command system requires written plans whenever 25. ____

    I. resources from multiple agencies are used
    II. the incident involves hazardous materials
    III. the incident requires changes in personnel shifts or equipment
    IV. multiple jurisdictions are involved

A. I and IV
B. I, III and IV
C. III and IV
D. I, II, III and IV

KEY (CORRECT ANSWERS)

1. D
2. C
3. D
4. D
5. A

6. C
7. C
8. B
9. C
10. C

11. B
12. D
13. B
14. A
15. C

16. D
17. A
18. A
19. A
20. C

21. A
22. A
23. C
24. B
25. B

13) The incident command system designates the ideal number of subordi-   13. _____
nates to serve under a single supervisor during an incident as

A. 3
B. 5
C. 8
D. 12

14) In the financial management of a disaster at the federal level, which of   14. _____
the following would typically be performed LAST?

A. The program office requests deobligation of excess funds not needed.
B. The allocation for the program is processed at FEMA headquarters
C. A grantee draws down funds
D. The program office prepares a worksheet to amend the initial allocation.

15) A community that wants to obtain aid for comprehensive mitigation   15. _____
planning should contact

A. FEMA
B. the state's NFIP liaison
C. the state's hazard mitigation officer
D. the state's office of emergency preparedness

16) Which element of an emergency team includes all twelve of the feder-   16. _____
ally-defined emergency support functions (ESFs)?

A. Logistics
B. Mission Assignment
C. Mobile Emergency Response System (MERS)
D. Operations

17) In the financial management of a disaster, "drawdown" refers to the   17. _____

A. process of requesting and receiving payments into a grantee's account
B. downward adjustment of a previously recorded obligation
C. process of setting aside funds for a specific program
D. formal reservation of funds

18) Which of the following is not a "disaster-dependent" program?   18. _____

A. Flood Mitigation Assistance Program
B. Community Rating System
C. Metropolitan Medical Response Service
D. National Flood Insurance Program

19) Under the incident command system, three patrol units assigned to maintain crowd control would be defined as a

A. strike team
B. section
C. division
D. task force

20) Which of the following would be considered "permanent" work at a disaster site?

A. Construction of a temporary bridge span over a flooding river or stream
B. Installation of generators to provide power at public schools and hospitals
C. Installation of seismic retrofits in older structures
D. Debris clearance

21) _____ percent of public disaster assistance is assumed by the state(s) in which the disaster has occurred.

A. 25
B. 50
C. 75
D. 100

22) Ideally, the reconstruction of hazard-damaged structures should be accompanied by

A. the adoption or augmentation of building codes to minimize risk
B. strict land use controls
C. greater percentage allowances for state and federal hazard mitigation funds to the structure's owner or owners
D. increased insurance premiums

23) During the initial weeks of an emergency response, an "operational period" is typically _____ hours.

A. 8
B. 12
C. 24
D. 48

EXAMINATION SECTION
TEST 1

DIRECTIONS: Each question or incomplete statement is followed by several suggested answers or completions. Select the one that BEST answers the question or completes the statement. *PRINT THE LETTER OF THE CORRECT ANSWER IN THE SPACE AT THE RIGHT.*

1. In public agencies, communications should be based PRIMARILY on a

    A. two-way flow from the top down and from the bottom up, most of which should be given in writing to avoid ambiguity
    B. multidirection flow among all levels and with outside persons
    C. rapid, internal one-way flow from the top down
    D. two-way flow of information, most of which should be given orally for purposes of clarity

    1.____

2. In some organizations, changes in policy or procedures are often communicated by word of mouth from supervisors to employees with no prior discussion or exchange of viewpoints with employees.
   This procedure often produces employee dissatisfaction CHIEFLY because

    A. information is mostly unusable since a considerable amount of time is required to transmit information
    B. lower-level supervisors tend to be excessively concerned with minor details
    C. management has failed to seek employees' advice before making changes
    D. valuable staff time is lost between decision-making and the implementation of decisions

    2.____

3. For good letter writing, you should try to visualize the person to whom you are writing, especially if you know him.
   Of the following rules, it is LEAST helpful in such visualization to think of

    A. the person's likes and dislikes, his concerns, and his needs
    B. what you would be likely to say if speaking in person
    C. what you would expect to be asked if speaking in person
    D. your official position in order to be certain that your words are proper

    3.____

4. One approach to good informal letter writing is to make letters sound conversational.
   All of the following practices will usually help to do this EXCEPT:

    A. If possible, use a style which is similar to the style used when speaking
    B. Substitute phrases for single words (e.g., *at the present time* for *now*)
    C. Use contractions of words (e.g., *you're* for *you are*)
    D. Use ordinary vocabulary when possible

    4.____

5. All of the following rules will aid in producing clarity in report-writing EXCEPT:

    A. Give specific details or examples, if possible
    B. Keep related words close together in each sentence
    C. Present information in sequential order
    D. Put several thoughts or ideas in each paragraph

    5.____

6. The one of the following statements about public relations which is MOST accurate is that
   A. in the long run, appearance gains better results than performance
   B. objectivity is decreased if outside public relations consultants are employed
   C. public relations is the responsibility of every employee
   D. public relations should be based on a formal publicity program

7. The form of communication which is usually considered to be MOST personally directed to the intended recipient is the
   A. brochure   B. film   C. letter   D. radio

8. In general, a document that presents an organization's views or opinions on a particular topic is MOST accurately known as a
   A. tear sheet
   B. position paper
   C. flyer
   D. journal

9. Assume that you have been asked to speak before an organization of persons who oppose a newly announced program in which you are involved. You feel tense about talking to this group.
   Which of the following rules generally would be MOST useful in gaining rapport when speaking before the audience?
   A. Impress them with your experience
   B. Stress all areas of disagreement
   C. Talk to the group as to one person
   D. Use formal grammar and language

10. An organization must have an effective public relations program since, at its best, public relations is a bridge to change.
    All of the following statements about communication and human behavior have validity EXCEPT:
    A. People are more likely to talk about controversial matters with like-minded people than with those holding other views
    B. The earlier an experience, the more powerful its effect since it influences how later experiences will be interpreted
    C. In periods of social tension, official sources gain increased believability
    D. Those who are already interested in a topic are the ones who are most open to receive new communications about it

11. An employee should be encouraged to talk easily and frankly when he is dealing with his supervisor.
    In order to encourage such free communication, it would be MOST appropriate for a supervisor to behave in a(n)
    A. sincere manner; assure the employee that you will deal with him honestly and openly
    B. official manner; you are a supervisor and must always act formally with subordinates

C. investigative manner; you must probe and question to get to a basis of trust
D. unemotional manner; the employee's emotions and background should play no part in your dealings with him

12. Research findings show that an increase in free communication within an agency GENERALLY results in which one of the following?

   A. Improved morale and productivity
   B. Increased promotional opportunities
   C. An increase in authority
   D. A spirit of honesty

13. Assume that you are a supervisor and your superiors have given you a new-type procedure to be followed.
Before passing this information on to your subordinates, the one of the following actions that you should take FIRST is to

   A. ask your superiors to send out a memorandum to the entire staff
   B. clarify the procedure in your own mind
   C. set up a training course to provide instruction on the new procedure
   D. write a memorandum to your subordinates

14. Communication is necessary for an organization to be effective.
The one of the following which is LEAST important for most communication systems is that

   A. messages are sent quickly and directly to the person who needs them to operate
   B. information should be conveyed understandably and accurately
   C. the method used to transmit information should be kept secret so that security can be maintained
   D. senders of messages must know how their messages are received and acted upon

15. Which one of the following is the CHIEF advantage of listening willingly to subordinates and encouraging them to talk freely and honestly?
It

   A. reveals to supervisors the degree to which ideas that are passed down are accepted by subordinates
   B. reduces the participation of subordinates in the operation of the department
   C. encourages subordinates to try for promotion
   D. enables supervisors to learn more readily what the *grapevine* is saying

16. A supervisor may be informed through either oral or written reports.
Which one of the following is an ADVANTAGE of using oral reports?

   A. There is no need for a formal record of the report.
   B. An exact duplicate of the report is not easily transmitted to others.
   C. A good oral report requires little time for preparation.
   D. An oral report involves two-way communication between a subordinate and his supervisor.

17. Of the following, the MOST important reason why supervisors should communicate effectively with the public is to

   A. improve the public's understanding of information that is important for them to know
   B. establish a friendly relationship
   C. obtain information about the kinds of people who come to the agency
   D. convince the public that services are adequate

18. Supervisors should generally NOT use phrases like *too hard*, *too easy*, and *a lot* PRINCIPALLY because such phrases

   A. may be offensive to some minority groups
   B. are too informal
   C. mean different things to different people
   D. are difficult to remember

19. The ability to communicate clearly and concisely is an important element in effective leadership.
   Which of the following statements about oral and written communication is GENERALLY true?

   A. Oral communication is more time-consuming.
   B. Written communication is more likely to be misinterpreted.
   C. Oral communication is useful only in emergencies.
   D. Written communication is useful mainly when giving information to fewer than twenty people.

20. Rumors can often have harmful and disruptive effects on an organization.
   Which one of the following is the BEST way to prevent rumors from becoming a problem?

   A. Refuse to act on rumors, thereby making them less believable.
   B. Increase the amount of information passed along by the *grapevine*.
   C. Distribute as much factual information as possible.
   D. Provide training in report writing.

21. Suppose that a subordinate asks you about a rumor he has heard. The rumor deals with a subject which your superiors consider *confidential*.
   Which of the following BEST describes how you should answer the subordinate?
   Tell

   A. the subordinate that you don't make the rules and that he should speak to higher ranking officials
   B. the subordinate that you will ask your superior for information
   C. him only that you cannot comment on the matter
   D. him the rumor is not true

22. Supervisors often find it difficult to *get their message across* when instructing newly appointed employees in their various duties.
   The MAIN reason for this is generally that the

A. duties of the employees have increased
B. supervisor is often so expert in his area that he fails to see it from the learner's point of view
C. supervisor adapts his instruction to the slowest learner in the group
D. new employees are younger, less concerned with job security and more interested in fringe benefits

23. Assume that you are discussing a job problem with an employee under your supervision. During the discussion, you see that the man's eyes are turning away from you and that he is not paying attention.
In order to get the man's attention, you should FIRST

   A. ask him to look you in the eye
   B. talk to him about sports
   C. tell him he is being very rude
   D. change your tone of voice

24. As a supervisor, you may find it necessary to conduct meetings with your subordinates. Of the following, which would be MOST helpful in assuring that a meeting accomplishes the purpose for which it was called?

   A. Give notice of the conclusions you would like to reach at the start of the meeting.
   B. Delay the start of the meeting until everyone is present.
   C. Write down points to be discussed in proper sequence.
   D. Make sure everyone is clear on whatever conclusions have been reached and on what must be done after the meeting.

25. Every supervisor will occasionally be called upon to deliver a reprimand to a subordinate. If done properly, this can greatly help an employee improve his performance.
Which one of the following is NOT a good practice to follow when giving a reprimand?

   A. Maintain your composure and temper.
   B. Reprimand a subordinate in the presence of other employees so they can learn the same lesson.
   C. Try to understand why the employee was not able to perform satisfactorily.
   D. Let your knowledge of the man involved determine the exact nature of the reprimand.

KEY (CORRECT ANSWERS)

1.	C	11.	A
2.	B	12.	A
3.	D	13.	B
4.	B	14.	C
5.	D	15.	A
6.	C	16.	D
7.	C	17.	A
8.	B	18.	C
9.	C	19.	B
10.	C	20.	C

21. B
22. B
23. D
24. D
25. B

TEST 2

DIRECTIONS: Each question or incomplete statement is followed by several suggested answers or completions. Select the one that BEST answers the question or completes the statement. *PRINT THE LETTER OF THE CORRECT ANSWER IN THE SPACE AT THE RIGHT.*

1. Usually one thinks of communication as a single step, essentially that of transmitting an idea.
   Actually, however, this is only part of a total process, the FIRST step of which should be

   A. the prompt dissemination of the idea to those who may be affected by it
   B. motivating those affected to take the required action
   C. clarifying the idea in one's own mind
   D. deciding to whom the idea is to be communicated

2. Research studies on patterns of informal communication have concluded that most individuals in a group tend to be passive recipients of news, while a few make it their business to spread it around in an organization.
   With this conclusion in mind, it would be MOST correct for the supervisor to attempt to identify these few individuals and

   A. give them the complete facts on important matters in advance of others
   B. inform the other subordinates of the identify of these few individuals so that their influence may be minimized
   C. keep them straight on the facts on important matters
   D. warn them to cease passing along any information to others

3. The one of the following which is the PRINCIPAL advantage of making an oral report is that it

   A. affords an immediate opportunity for two-way communication between the subordinate and superior
   B. is an easy method for the superior to use in transmitting information to others of equal rank
   C. saves the time of all concerned
   D. permits more precise pinpointing of praise or blame by means of follow-up questions by the superior

4. An agency may sometimes undertake a public relations program of a defensive nature.
   With reference to the use of defensive public relations, it would be MOST correct to state that it

   A. is bound to be ineffective since defensive statements, even though supported by factual data, can never hope to even partly overcome the effects of prior unfavorable attacks
   B. proves that the agency has failed to establish good relationships with newspapers, radio stations, or other means of publicity
   C. shows that the upper echelons of the agency have failed to develop sound public relations procedures and techniques
   D. is sometimes required to aid morale by protecting the agency from unjustified criticism and misunderstanding of policies or procedures

5. Of the following factors which contribute to possible undesirable public attitudes towards an agency, the one which is MOST susceptible to being changed by the efforts of the individual employee in an organization is that

   A. enforcement of unpopular regulations has offended many individuals
   B. the organization itself has an unsatisfactory reputation
   C. the public is not interested in agency matters
   D. there are many errors in judgment committed by individual subordinates

6. It is not enough for an agency's services to be of a high quality; attention must also be given to the acceptability of these services to the general public.
   This statement is GENERALLY

   A. *false;* a superior quality of service automatically wins public support
   B. *true;* the agency cannot generally progress beyond the understanding and support of the public
   C. *false;* the acceptance by the public of agency services determines their quality
   D. *true;* the agency is generally unable to engage in any effective enforcement activity without public support

7. Sustained agency participation in a program sponsored by a community organization is MOST justified when

   A. the achievement of agency objectives in some area depends partly on the activity of this organization
   B. the community organization is attempting to widen the base of participation in all community affairs
   C. the agency is uncertain as to what the community wants
   D. there is an obvious lack of good leadership in a newly formed community organization

8. Of the following, the LEAST likely way in which a records system may serve a supervisor is in

   A. developing a sympathetic and cooperative public attitude toward the agency
   B. improving the quality of supervision by permitting a check on the accomplishment of subordinates
   C. permit a precise prediction of the exact incidences in specific categories for the following year
   D. helping to take the guesswork out of the distribution of the agency

9. Assuming that the *grapevine* in any organization is virtually indestructible, the one of the following which it is MOST important for management to understand is:

   A. What is being spread by means of the *grapevine* and the reason for spreading it
   B. What is being spread by means of the *grapevine* and how it is being spread
   C. Who is involved in spreading the information that is on the *grapevine*
   D. Why those who are involved in spreading the information are doing so

10. When the supervisor writes a report concerning an investigation to which he has been assigned, it should be LEAST intended to provide

   A. a permanent official record of relevant information gathered
   B. a summary of case findings limited to facts which tend to indicate the guilt of a suspect
   C. a statement of the facts on which higher authorities may base a corrective or disciplinary action
   D. other investigators with information so that they may continue with other phases of the investigation

11. In survey work, questionnaires rather than interviews are sometimes used.
   The one of the following which is a DISADVANTAGE of the questionnaire method as compared with the interview is the

   A. difficulty of accurately interpreting the results
   B. problem of maintaining anonymity of the participant
   C. fact that it is relatively uneconomical
   D. requirement of special training for the distribution of questionnaires

12. In his contacts with the public, an employee should attempt to create a good climate of support for his agency. This statement is GENERALLY

   A. *false;* such attempts are clearly beyond the scope of his responsibility
   B. *true;* employees of an agency who come in contact with the public have the opportunity to affect public relations
   C. *false;* such activity should be restricted to supervisors trained in public relations techniques
   D. *true;* the future expansion of the agency depends to a great extent on continued public support of the agency

13. The repeated use by a supervisor of a call for volunteers to get a job done is objectionable MAINLY because it

   A. may create a feeling of animosity between the volunteers and the non-volunteers
   B. may indicate that the supervisor is avoiding responsibility for making assignments which will be most productive
   C. is an indication that the supervisor is not familiar with the individual capabilities of his men
   D. is unfair to men who, for valid reasons, do not, or cannot volunteer

14. Of the following statements concerning subordinates' expressions to a supervisor of their opinions and feelings concerning work situations, the one which is MOST correct is that

   A. by listening and responding to such expressions the supervisor encourages the development of complaints
   B. the lack of such expressions should indicate to the supervisor that there is a high level of job satisfaction
   C. the more the supervisor listens to and responds to such expressions, the more he demonstrates lack of supervisory ability
   D. by listening and responding to such expressions, the supervisor will enable many subordinates to understand and solve their own problems on the job

15. In attempting to motivate employees, rewards are considered preferable to punishment PRIMARILY because

    A. punishment seldom has any effect on human behavior
    B. punishment usually results in decreased production
    C. supervisors find it difficult to punish
    D. rewards are more likely to result in willing cooperation

16. In an attempt to combat the low morale in his organization, a high-level supervisor publicized an *open-door* policy to allow employees who wished to do so to come to him with their complaints.
    Which of the following is LEAST likely to account for the fact that no employee came in with a complaint?

    A. Employees are generally reluctant to go over the heads of their immediate supervisors.
    B. The employees did not feel that management would help them.
    C. The low morale was not due to complaints associated with the job.
    D. The employees felt that they had more to lose than to gain.

17. It is MOST desirable to use written instructions rather than oral instructions for a particular job when

    A. a mistake on the job will not be serious
    B. the job can be completed in a short time
    C. there is no need to explain the job minutely
    D. the job involves many details

18. If you receive a telephone call regarding a matter which your office does not handle, you should FIRST

    A. give the caller the telephone number of the proper office so that he can dial again
    B. offer to transfer the caller to the proper office
    C. suggest that the caller re-dial since he probably dialed incorrectly
    D. tell the caller he has reached the wrong office and then hang up

19. When you answer the telephone, the MOST important reason for identifying yourself and your organization is to

    A. give the caller time to collect his or her thoughts
    B. impress the caller with your courtesy
    C. inform the caller that he or she has reached the right number
    D. set a business-like tone at the beginning of the conversation

20. As soon as you pick up the phone, a very angry caller begins immediately to complain about city agencies and *red tape*. He says that he has been shifted to two or three different offices. It turns out that he is seeking information which is not immediately available to you. You believe you know, however, where it can be found. Which of the following actions is the BEST one for you to take?

    A. To eliminate all confusion, suggest that the caller write the agency stating explicitly what he wants.
    B. Apologize by telling the caller how busy city agencies now are, but also tell him directly that you do not have the information he needs.

C. Ask for the caller's telephone number and assure him you will call back after you have checked further.
D. Give the caller the name and telephone number of the person who might be able to help, but explain that you are not positive he will get results.

21. Which of the following approaches usually provides the BEST communication in the objectives and values of a new program which is to be introduced?

   A. A general written description of the program by the program manager for review by those who share responsibility
   B. An effective verbal presentation by the program manager to those affected
   C. Development of the plan and operational approach in carrying out the program by the program manager assisted by his key subordinates
   D. Development of the plan by the program manager's supervisor

21.____

22. What is the BEST approach for introducing change?
A

   A. combination of written and also verbal communication to all personnel affected by the change
   B. general bulletin to all personnel
   C. meeting pointing out all the values of the new approach
   D. written directive to key personnel

22.____

23. Of the following, committees are BEST used for

   A. advising the head of the organization
   B. improving functional work
   C. making executive decisions
   D. making specific planning decisions

23.____

24. An effective discussion leader is one who

   A. announces the problem and his preconceived solution at the start of the discussion
   B. guides and directs the discussion according to pre-arranged outline
   C. interrupts or corrects confused participants to save time
   D. permits anyone to say anything at anytime

24.____

25. The human relations movement in management theory is basically concerned with

   A. counteracting employee unrest
   B. eliminating the *time and motion* man
   C. interrelationships among individuals in organizations
   D. the psychology of the worker

25.____

KEY (CORRECT ANSWERS)

1.	C		11.	A
2.	C		12.	B
3.	A		13.	B
4.	D		14.	D
5.	D		15.	D
6.	B		16.	C
7.	A		17.	D
8.	C		18.	B
9.	A		19.	C
10.	B		20.	C

21. C
22. A
23. A
24. B
25. C

EXAMINATION SECTION
TEST 1

Directions: Each question or incomplete statement is followed by several suggested answers or completions. Select the one that BEST answers the question or completes the statement. *PRINT THE LETTER OF THE CORRECT ANSWER IN THE SPACE AT THE RIGHT.*

1) A specialist is meeting with a panel of local community leaders to determine their perceptions about the effectiveness of a recent outreach program. The leaders seem unresponsive to the specialist's questions, looking at the floor or each other without directly answering the specialist's questions. One strategy that might work to elicit the desired information would be to

A. try to discern the hidden meaning of their silence
B. adopt a mildly confrontational tone and remind them of what's at stake in the community
C. keep asking open-ended questions and wait patiently for responses
D. tell them to come back when they're ready to tell you their opinions

1._____

2) Each of the following statements about maintaining a community's attention is true, EXCEPT

A. The more challenging it is to pay attention to a message, the more likely it is that it will be attended to.
B. Listeners will be more motivated to pay attention if a speech is personally meaningful.
C. People will be more likely to attend if a speaker pauses to suggest natural transitions in a speech.
D. Listeners will attend to messages that stand out.

2._____

3) Each of the following is a key strategy to integrative bargaining among community members in conflict, EXCEPT

A. focusing on positions, rather than interests
B. separating the people from the problem
C. aiming for an outcome based on an objectively identified standard
D. using active listening skills, such as rephrasing and questioning

3._____

4) Which of the following is NOT one of the major variables to take into account when considering a community needs assessment?

A. State of program development
B. Resources available
C. Demographics
D. Community attitudes

4._____

5) Which of the following groups would probably be formed specifically for, or be involved in, the purpose of addressing a specific unmet community need?

A. An existing consumer group
B. A council of community representatives
C. A committee
D. An existing community organization

6) If a public outreach campaign designed to mobilize a community fails, the most likely reason for this failure is that the campaign

A. was not specific about what they want people to do
B. are overly serious and do not appeal to people's sense of humor
C. offered no incentive for the audience to make a change
D. did not use language that appealed to the audience's emotions

7) Nationwide, the rate of involvement of elderly people in community-based programs demonstrates that they are

A. underserved when compared to other age groups
B. served at about the same rate as other age groups
C. over-served when compared to other age groups
D. hardly served at all

8) In projecting the likelihood of an education program's success, a domestic violence specialist identifies every single event that must occur to complete the project. The specialist then arranges these events in sequential order and allocates time requirements for each. Finally, the total time is calculated and a model showing all their events and timelines is charted. The specialist has used

A. a PERT chart
B. a simulation
C. a Markov model
D. the critical path method

9) When working with members of a predominantly African-American community, specialists from other cultural backgrounds should be aware that African Americans tend to express thoughts and feelings through descriptions of

A. physically tangible sensations
B. problems to be analyzed
C. corresponding analogies
D. spiritual issues

10) Local nonprofessionals should be considered useful to a specialist who is looking to undertake a community outreach or educational initiative. Which of the following is LEAST likely to be a characteristic or role demonstrated by these community members?

10. _____

A. Undertaking support functions at the agency
B. Serving as a communication channel between the agency and clients
C. Encouraging greater agency acceptance and credibility within the community
D. Helping the agency to accomplish meaningful change

11) In working with Native American groups or clients, it is important to recognize that the greatest health problem facing their communities today is

11. _____

A. domestic violence
B. depression and suicide
C. alcoholism
D. tuberculosis

12) A specialist is facilitating a cooperative conflict resolution session between community members who have different opinions about what kinds of intervention services should be offered by the local adult protective services agency. Which of the following is NOT a guideline that should be followed in this process?

12. _____

A. Early in the negotiations, ask each party to name the issues on which they will positively not yield.
B. Try to get the parties to view the issue from other points of view, beside the two or three conflicting ones.
C. Have each side volunteer what it would be willing to do to resolve the conflict.
D. At the end of the session, draw up a formal agreement with agreed-upon actions for both parties.

13) A specialist wants to evaluate the effectiveness of a local women's shelter. The shelter has suffered from lax participation, given the number of women who have been abused in the surrounding area. The specialist wants to speak with the women in the community who did not follow up on referrals to the shelter, and begins by visiting some of these women. After gaining the trust of these women, the specialist asks for the names of women they know who might be in need of help with a domestic violence situation. The specialist's approach in this case is _____ sampling.

13. _____

A. maximum variation
B. snowball
C. convenience
D. typical case

14) When it comes to perceiving messages, people typically DON'T   14. ____

A. tend to simplify causal connections and sometimes even seek a single cause to explain what may be a highly complex effect
B. tend to perceive messages independently of a categorical framework, especially if the message may be distorted by such an interpretation
C. have a predisposition toward accepting any pattern that a speaker offers to explain seemingly unconnected facts
D. tend to interpret things in the way they are viewed by their reference group

15) The elder members of Native American communities, regardless of kinship, are most commonly referred to as   15. ____

A. the ancients
B. father or mother
C. grandfather or grandmother
D. chiefs

16) Each of the following is typically an objective of community mobilization, EXCEPT   16. ____

A. To convince existing community resources to alter their services or work together to address an unmet need
B. To gather and distribute information to consumers and agencies about unmet needs
C. To publicize existing community resources and make them more accessible
D. To bring an unmet community need to public attention in order to achieve acceptance of and support for fulfilling the need

17) Research in community outreach shows that women often build friendships through shared positive feelings, whereas men often build friendships through   17. ____

A. metacommunication
B. catharsis
C. impression management
D. shared activities

18) Typically, the FIRST step in a community needs assessment is to   18. ____

A. identify community's strengths
B. explore the nature of the neighborhood
C. get to know the area and its residents
D. talk to people in the community

19) Most public relations experts agree that _____ exposure(s) to a message is the minimum just to get the message noticed. If the aim of a public outreach campaign is action or a change in behavior, the agency budget must plan for more exposures.

19. _____

A. one
B. two
C. three
D. four

20) In the program development/community liaison model of community work and public outreach, the primary constituency is considered to be

20. _____

A. community representatives and the service agency board or administrators
B. elected officials, social agencies, and interagency organizations
C. marginalized or oppressed population groups in a city or region
D. residents of a neighborhood, parish or rural county

21) Social or interpersonal problems in many African American communities have their roots in

21. _____

A. personality deficits
B. unresolved family conflicts
C. poor communication
D. external stressors

22) A public outreach campaign should

22. _____

I. focus on short-term, measurable goals, rather than ultimate outcomes
II. try to alter entrenched attitudes within a short time, with powerfully worded messages
III. proceed in steps or phases, each of which lays out a mechanism that leads to the desired effect
IV. ignore causes that led to a problem, and instead focus on solutions

A. I and II
B. II and III
C. III only
D. I, II, III and IV

23) Research findings indicate that in listing preferences for helping professional attributes, individuals from culturally diverse groups are MOST likely to _____ as more important than _____.

A. personality similarity; either race/ethnic similarity or attitude similarity
B. therapist experience; any kind of similarity
C. race/ethnic similarity; attitude similarity
D. attitude similarity; race/ethnic similarity

24) Each of the following is considered to be an objective of community organization, EXCEPT

A. effecting changes in the distribution of decision-making power
B. helping people develop and strengthen the traits of self-direction and cooperation
C. effecting and maintaining the balance between needs and resources in a community
D. helping people deal with their problems by developing alternative behaviors

25) A specialist is helping the adult protective services agency to design a public outreach campaign. The topic to be addressed is complex, public understanding is low, and most professionals at the agency feel that having more complete information might change the opinions of community members. Which method of pre-campaign research is probably most appropriate?

A. Deliberative polling
B. Attitude scales
C. Surveys or questionnaires
D. Focus groups

KEY (CORRECT ANSWERS)

1. C
2. A
3. A
4. C
5. C

6. A
7. A
8. D
9. C
10. A

11. C
12. A
13. B
14. B
15. C

16. B
17. D
18. B
19. C
20. A

21. D
22. C
23. D
24. D
25. A

TEST 2

Directions: Each question or incomplete statement is followed by several suggested answers or completions. Select the one the BEST answers the question or completes the statement. *PRINT THE LETTER OF THE CORRECT ANSWER IN THE SPACE AT THE RIGHT.*

1) A specialist has been called in to resolve a dispute between two community leaders who have been arguing about the level of service needed within the community. The discussion has been going on for several hours when the specialist arrives, and both people seem to be upset. After calming the two down and getting each of them to agree on a statement of the problem, the specialist should ask each person to

1. _____

A. summarize his or her argument in three main points
B. explain why he or she became so upset
C. clearly state, in objective terms, the position of the other in a form that meets with the other's approval
D. identify the best alternative outcome, other than their presumed ideal

2) In evaluation the impact of a public outreach campaign, the _____ model can be used early in he campaign to address first impressions.

2. _____

A. exposure or advertising
B. expert interview
C. impact monitoring or process
D. experimental or quasi-experimental

3) When trying to motivate an older population to take action on a community problem, it is helpful to remember that older people

3. _____

A. are more self-reliant in their decision-making than other members of the same family
B. often need more time to decide than younger people
C. are more likely than younger people to view community problems self-referentially
D. tend to take a pragmatic, rather than philosophical, view of life

4) The method of group or community decision-making that is normally most time-consuming is

4. _____

A. majority opinion
B. consensus
C. expert opinion
D. authority rule

5) A local adult protective services agency has identified one of the goals of its recent public outreach campaign to be the mobilization of activists. The campaign should probably

A. target neutral audiences
B. home in on supporters
C. stick to purely factual information
D. try to persuade community fence-sitters

6) Research of Native American youths' perceptions of family concerns for their well-being has generally found that these youths

A. have a high degree of uncertainty about their families' feelings toward them
B. believe their families don't care about them
C. believe that their mothers care a great deal about them, but their fathers don't
D. believe their families care a great deal about them

7) A domestic violence specialist is developing a new outreach program for the local community. The specialist has defined the target problem, set program goals, and planned the actions that will take place as a result of the program. Most likely, the next step will be to

A. evaluate the resources available to achieve program goals
B. define and sequence the steps that will be taken to achieve program goals
C. determine how the program will be evaluated
D. decide how the program will operate

8) In the following exchange, what listening skill is evident in the underlined statement?

Elder: *I'm so glad to have someone to talk to, someone who really understands my problem.*

Specialist: <u>It is nice to be able to talk to someone who will listen</u>.

Elder: That's for sure.

A. verbatim response
B. paraphrasing
C. advising
D. evaluation

9) Which of the following activities is involved in the specialist's task of mobilizing?

A. Meeting individuals in the community with problems and assisting them in finding help
B. Identifying unmet community needs
C. Speaking out against an unjust policy or procedure
D. Developing new services or linking presently available services to meet community needs

9. _____

10) The preliminary research associated with a public outreach campaign should FIRST be aimed at determining

A. the budget
B. the message's ultimate audience
C. what media to use
D. the short-term behavioral goals of the campaign

10. _____

11) A specialist in a low-income community wants to plan programs that will deal with the influence of unemployment on domestic disturbances. The specialist needs to know not only how many unemployed people are in the community now, but also how many people will be unemployed at any particular time in the future, and how those numbers will vary given certain conditions. Probably the best way to trace employment rates over time and within differing conditions is through the use of

A. the critical path method
B. linear programming
C. difference equations
D. the Markov model

11. _____

12) Generally, public outreach programs—whatever their stated goal—should

    I. create a sense of urgency about a problem
    II. decline to identify opponents of the issue or idea
    III. propose concrete, easily understandable solutions
    IV. urge a specific action

A. I only
B. I, III and IV
C. II and III
D. I, II, III and IV

12. _____

13) Which of the following methods of community needs assessment relies to the greatest degree on existing public records?

A. Social indicators
B. Field study
C. Rates-under treatment
D. Key informant

14) During an interview with a Native American client, a specialist is careful to maintain close and nearly constant eye contact. The client is most likely to interpret this as

A. a show of high concern
B. a sign of disrespect
C. an uncomfortable assumption of intimacy
D. an attempt to intimidate

15) The best strategy for addressing an audience that is known to be captive, or even hostile, is to

A. refer to experiences in common
B. flatter the audience
C. joke about things in or near the audience
D. plead for fairness

16) Integrative conflict resolution is characterized by

A. an overriding concern to maximize joint outcomes
B. one side's interests opposing the other's
C. a fixed and limited amount of resources to be divided, so that the more one group gets, the less another gets
D. manipulation and withholding information as negotiation strategies

17) A specialist wants to learn how to interact with the members of a largely Latino community in a more culturally sensitive way. Which of the following is NOT a guideline for interacting with members of a Latino community?

A. Efforts to foster independence and self-reliance may be interpreted by many Latinos as a lack of concern for others.
B. Efforts to deal one-on-one with an adolescent client may serve to alienate the parents, especially the mother.
C. A nonverbal gesture such as lowering the eyes is interpreted by many Latinos as a sign of respect and deference to authority.
D. In much of Latino culture, the locus of control for problems tends to be much more external than internal.

18) Each of the following is an supporting assumption of community organization, EXCEPT

A. democracy requires cooperative participation
B. in order for communities to change, it is necessary for each individual in the community to be willing to change
C. communities often need help with organization and planning
D. holistic approaches work better than fragmented or ad-hoc programs

19) Helping professionals often have difficulty to bring community resources together to fulfill unmet community needs. Which of the following is NOT usually a reason for this?

A. Some community groups resist assistance when it is offered.
B. Few community groups make their needs known.
C. Community resources frequently change the type of services they offer.
D. Often, community resources prefer to work alone

20) When dealing with groups or populations of elderly clients, specialists should be mindful that about _____ of the nation's elderly suffer from mental health problems.

A. a tenth
B. a quarter
C. a third
D. half

21) In an African American community, a specialist from another culture should recognize that church participation, for most African Americans, is viewed as a

A. method for maintaining control and communicating competency
B. way of depersonalizing problems or troubles
C. way to divert attention away from problems
D. means of cathartic emotional release

22) Adult protective service programs supported by state statutes protect elderly people from abuse and neglect under the doctrine of

A. parens patriae
B. habeas corpus
C. in loco parentis
D. volenti non fit injuria

23) In terms of public outreach, which of the following statements about an audience is NOT generally true?

23. _____

A. The more heterogeneous the audience, the more necessary it will be to use specific examples and appeals to certain types of people
B. The smaller the audience, the more likely that its members will share assumptions and values
C. When the speaker does not know the status of an audience, it is best to assume that they are captive rather than voluntary
D. The larger an audience, the more formal a presentation is likely to be

24) A specialist often spends time in the places frequented by community residents. She listens carefully to what residents seem most concerned about, and engages many in conversations, asking them how they see the problems in the community. During these conversations, she makes mental notes about whether the statements of the problems are the same things that are mentioned in their conversations. From these conversations, the worker determines what she thinks the unmet needs of the community are. Which of the key issues in identifying unmet needs has the worker neglected to address?

24. _____

A. The different points of view regarding the issues, and whether there is any common ground.
B. Whether the stated problems and the conversations with community residents reflect the same concerns.
C. How community residents define the issues.
D. What the residents talk about with one another in a community.

25) Which of the following political styles should be used to promote an issue that could become controversial if it is perceived to involve major reforms?

25. _____

A. High-conflict, polarized
B. High-conflict, consensual
C. Moderate conflict, compromise-oriented
D. Low-conflict, technical

KEY (CORRECT ANSWERS)

1. C
2. A
3. B
4. B
5. B

6. D
7. A
8. B
9. D
10. B

11. D
12. B
13. A
14. B
15. A

16. A
17. D
18. B
19. C
20. B

21. D
22. A
23. A
24. A
25. D

EXAMINATION SECTION

DIRECTIONS FOR THIS SECTION:
Each question or incomplete statement is followed by several suggested answers or completions. Select the one that BEST answer the question or completes the statement. *PRINT THE LETTER OF THE CORRECT ANSWER IN THE SPACE AT THE RIGHT.*

TEST 1

1. Although some kinds of instructions are best put in written form, a supervisor can give many instructions verbally. In which one of the following situations would verbal instructions be MOST suitable?
    A. Furnishing an employee with the details to be checked in doing a certain job
    B. Instructing an employee on the changes necessary to update the office manual used in your unit
    C. Informing a new employee where different kinds of supplies and equipment that he might need are kept
    D. Presenting an assignment to an employee who will be held accountable for following a series of steps

2. You may be asked to evaluate the organization structure of your unit. Which one of the following questions would you NOT expect to take up in an evaluation of this kind?
    A. Is there an employee whose personal problems are interfering with his or her work?
    B. Is there an up-to-date job description for each position in this section?
    C. Are related operations and tasks grouped together and regularly assigned together?
    D. Are responsibilities divided as far as possible, and is this division clearly understood by all employees?

3. In order to distribute and schedule work fairly and efficiently, a supervisor may wish to make a work distribution study. A simple way of getting the information necessary for such a study is to have everyone for one week keep track of each task done and the time spent on each. Which one of the following situations showing up in such a study would *most clearly* call for corrective action?
    A. The newest employee takes longer to do most tasks than do experienced employees
    B. One difficult operation takes longer to do than most other operations carried out by the section
    C. A particular employee is very frequently assigned tasks that are not similar and have no relationship to each other
    D. The most highly skilled employee is often assigned the most difficult jobs

4. The authority to carry out a job can be delegated to a subordinate, but the supervisor remains responsible for the work of the section as a whole. As a supervisor, which of the following rules would be the BEST one for you to follow in view of the above statement?
    A. Avoid assigning important tasks to your subordinates, because you will be blamed if anything goes wrong

1. ...

2. ...

3. ...

4. ...

B. Be sure each subordinate understands the specific job he has been assigned, and check at intervals to make sure assignments are done properly
C. Assign several people to every important job, so that responsibility will be spread out as much as possible
D. Have an experienced subordinate check all work done by other employees, so that there will be little chance of anything going wrong

5. The human tendency to resist change is often reflected in higher rates of turnover, absenteeism, and errors whenever an important change is made in an organization. Although psychologists do not fully understand the reasons why people resist change, they believe that the resistance stems from a threat to the individual's security, that it is a form of fear of the unknown.
In light of this statement, which one of the following approaches would probably be *MOST* effective in preparing employees for a change in procedure in their unit?   5. ...
   A. Avoid letting employees know anything about the change until the last possible moment
   B. Sympathize with employees who resent the change and let them know you share their doubts and fears
   C. Promise the employees that if the change turns out to be a poor one, you will allow them to suggest a return to the old system
   D. Make sure that employees know the reasons for the change and are aware of the benefits that are expected from it

6. Each of the following methods of encouraging employee participation in work planning has been used effectively with different kinds and sizes of employee groups.
Which one of the following methods would be *MOST* suitable for a group of four technically skilled employees?   6. ...
   A. Discussions between the supervisor and a representative of the group
   B. A suggestion program with semi-annual awards for outstanding suggestions
   C. A group discussion summoned whenever a major problem remains unsolved for more than a month
   D. Day-to-day exchange of information, opinions and experience

7. Of the following, the *MOST* important reason why a supervisor is given the authority to tell subordinates what work they should do, how they should do it, and when it should be done is that *usually*   7. ...
   A. most people will not work unless there is someone with authority standing over them
   B work is accomplished more effectively if the supervisor plans and coordinates it
   C. when division of work is left up to subordinates, there is constant arguing, and very little work is accomplished
   D. subordinates are not familiar with the tasks to be performed

8. Fatigue is a factor that affects productivity in all work situations. However, a brief rest period will ordinarily serve to restore a person from fatigue.   8. ...

According to this statement, which one of the following techniques is *most likely* to reduce the impact of fatigue on over-all productivity in a unit?
   A. Scheduling several short breaks throughout the day
   B. Allowing employees to go home early
   C. Extending the lunch period an extra half hour
   D. Rotating job assignments every few weeks

9. After giving a new task to an employee, it is a good idea for a supervisor to ask specific questions to make sure that the employee grasps the essentials of the task and sees how it can be carried out. Questions which ask the employee what he thinks or how he feels about an important aspect of the task are particularly effective.
Which one of the following questions is *NOT* the type of question which would be useful in the foregoing situation?
   A. "Do you feel there will be any trouble meeting the 4:30 deadline?"
   B. "How do you feel about the kind of work we do here?"
   C. "Do you think that combining those two steps will work all right?"
   D. "Can you think of any additional equipment you may need for this process?"

10. Of the following, the *LEAST* important reason for having a *continuous* training program is that
   A. employees may forget procedures that they have already learned
   B. employees may develop short cuts on the job that result in inaccurate work
   C. the job continues to change because of new procedures and equipment
   D. training is one means of measuring effectiveness and productivity on the job

11. In training a new employee, it is usually advisable to break down the job into meaningful parts and have the new employee master one part before going on to the next.
Of the following, the *BEST* reason for using this technique is to
   A. let the new employee know the reason for what he is doing and thus encourage him to remain in the unit
   B. make the employee aware of the importance of the work and encourage him to work harder
   C. show the employee that the work is easy so that he will be encouraged to work faster
   D. make it more likely that the employee will experience success and will be encouraged to continue learning the job

12. You may occasionally find a serious error in the work of one of your subordinates.
Of the following, the *BEST* time to discuss such an error with an employee *usually* is
   A. immediately after the error is found
   B. after about two weeks, since you will also be able to point out some good things that the employee has accomplished

C. when you have discovered a pattern of errors on the part of this employee so that he will not be able to dispute your criticism
D. after the error results in a complaint by your own supervisor

13. For very important announcements to the staff, a supervisor should usually use both written and oral communications. For example, when a new procedure is to be introduced, the supervisor can more easily obtain the group's acceptance by giving his subordinates a rough draft of the new procedure and calling a meeting of all his subordinates. The *LEAST* important benefit of this technique is that it will better enable the supervisor to
    A. explain why the change is necessary
    B. make adjustments in the new procedure to meet valid staff objections
    C. assign someone to carry out the new procedure
    D. answer questions about the new procedure

14. Assume that, while you are interviewing an individual to obtain information, the individual pauses in the middle of an answer.
    The *BEST* of the following actions for you to take at that time is to
    A. correct any inaccuracies in what he has said
    B. remain silent until he continues
    C. explain your position on the matter being discussed
    D. explain that time is short and that he must complete his story quickly

15. When you are interviewing someone to obtain information, the *BEST* of the following reasons for you to repeat certain of his exact words is to
    A. assure him that appropriate action will be taken
    B. encourage him to switch to another topic of discussion
    C. assure him that you agree with his point of view
    D. encourage him to elaborate on a point he has made

16. Generally, when writing a letter, the use of precise words and concise sentences is
    A. *good*, because less time will be required to write the letter
    B. *bad*, because it is most likely that the reader will think the letter is unimportant and will not respond favorably
    C. *good*, because it is likely that your desired meaning will be conveyed to the reader
    D. *bad*, because your letter will be too brief to provide adequate information

17. In which of the following cases would it be *MOST* desirable to have *two* cards for one individual in a *single* alphabetic file? The individual has
    A. a hyphenated surname   B. two middle names
    C. a first name with an unusual spelling
    D. a compound first name

18. Of the following, it is *MOST* appropriate to use a form letter when it is necessary to answer many
    A. requests or inquiries from a single individual

B. follow-up letters from individuals requesting additional information
C. requests or inquiries about a single subject
D. complaints from individuals that they have been unable to obtain various types of information

19. Assume that you are asked to make up a budget for your section for the coming year, and you are told that the most important function of the budget is its "control function."
Of the following, "control" in this context implies, *most nearly*, that
   A. you will probably be asked to justify expenditures in any category when it looks as though these expenditures are departing greatly from the amount budgeted
   B. your section will probably not be allowed to spend more than the budgeted amount in any given category, although it is always permissible to spend less
   C. your section will be required to spend the exact amount budgeted in every category
   D. the budget will be filed in the Office of the Comptroller so that when the year is over the actual expenditures can be compared with the amounts in the budget

20. In writing a report, the practice of taking up the *least* important points *first* and the *most* important points *last* is a
   A. *good technique* since the final points made in a report will make the greatest impression on the reader
   B. *good technique* since the material is presented in a more logical manner and will lead directly to the conclusions
   C. *poor technique* since the reader's time is wasted by having to review irrelevant information before finishing the report
   D. *poor technique* since it may cause the reader to lose interest in the report and arrive at incorrect conclusions about the report

21. Typically, when the technique of "supervision by results" is practiced, higher management sets down, either implicitly or explicitly, certain performance standards or goals that the subordinate is expected to meet. So long as these standards are met, management interferes very little.
The *most likely* result of the use of this technique is that it will
   A. lead to ambiguity in terms of goals
   B. be successful only to the extent that close direct supervision is practiced
   C. make it possible to evaluate both employee and supervisory effectiveness
   D. allow for complete dependence on the subordinate's part

22. When making written evaluations and reviews of the performance of subordinates, it is *usually ADVISABLE* to
   A. avoid informing the employee of the evaluation if it is critical because it may create hard feelings
   B. avoid informing the employee of the evaluation whether critical or favorable because it is tension-producing

C. to permit the employee to see the evaluation but not to discuss it with him because the supervisor cannot be certain where the discussion might lead
D. to discuss the evaluation openly with the employee because it helps the employee understand what is expected of him

23. There are a number of well-known and respected human relations principles that successful supervisors have been using for years in building good relationships with their employees. Which of the following does *NOT* illustrate such a principle?
    A. Give clear and complete instructions
    B. Let each person know how he is getting along
    C. Keep an open-door policy
    D. Make all relationships personal ones

24. Assume that it is necessary for you to give an unpleasant assignment to one of your subordinates. You expect this employee to raise some objections to this assignment.
The *most appropriate* of the following actions for you to take *FIRST* is to issue the assignment
    A. *orally*, with the further statement that you will not listen to any complaints
    B. *in writing*, to forestall any complaints by the employee
    C. *orally*, permitting the employee to express his feelings
    D. *in writing*, with a note that any comments should be submitted in writing

25. Suppose you have just announced at a staff meeting with your subordinates that a radical reorganization of work will take place next week. Your subordinates at the meeting appear to be excited, tense, and worried.
Of the following, the *BEST* action for you to take at that time is to
    A. schedule private conferences with each subordinate to obtain his reaction to the meeting
    B. close the meeting and tell your subordinates to return immediately to their work assignments
    C. give your subordinates some time to ask questions and discuss your announcement
    D. insist that your subordinates do not discuss your announcement among themselves or with other members of the agency

TEST 2

1. Of the following, the *BEST* way for a supervisor to increase employees' interest in their work is to
    A. allow them to make as many decisions as possible
    B. demonstrate to them that he is as technically competent as they
    C. give each employee a difficult assignment
    D. promptly convey to them instructions from higher management

2. The *one* of the following which is *LEAST* important in maintaining a high level of productivity on the part of employees is the

A. provision of optimum physical working conditions for employees
B. strength of employees' aspirations for promotion
C. anticipated satisfactions which employees hope to derive from their work
D. employees' interest in their jobs

3. Of the following, the *MAJOR* advantage of group problem-solving, as compared to individual problem-solving, is that groups will *more readily*
   A. abide by their own decisions
   B. agree with agency management
   C. devise new policies and procedures
   D. reach conclusions sooner

4. The group problem-solving conference is a useful supervisory method for getting people to reach solutions to problems.
   Of the following the *reason* that groups usually reach more realistic solutions than do individuals is that
   A. individuals, as a rule, take longer than do groups in reaching decisions and are therefore more likely to make an error
   B. bringing people together to let them confer impresses participants with the seriousness of problems
   C. groups are generally more concerned with the future in evaluating organizational problems
   D. the erroneous opinions of group members tend to be corrected by the other members

5. A competent supervisor should be able to distinguish between human and technical problems.
   Of the following, the *MAJOR* difference between such problems is that serious human problems, in comparison to ordinary technical problems,
   A. are remedied more quickly
   B. involve a lesser need for diagnosis
   C. are more difficult to define
   D. become known through indications which are usually the actual problem

6. Of the following, the *BEST* justification for a public agency establishing an alcoholism program for its employees is that
   A. alcoholism has traditionally been looked upon with a certain amused tolerance by management and thereby ignored as a serious illness
   B. employees with drinking problems have twice as many on-the-job accidents, especially during the early years of the problem
   C. excessive use of alcohol is associated with personality instability hindering informal social relationships among peers and subordinates
   D. the agency's public reputation will suffer despite an employee's drinking problem being a personal matter of little public concern

7. Assume you are a manager and you find a group of maintenance employees assigned to your project drinking and playing cards for money in an incinerator room after their regular working hours.

The one of the following actions it would be *BEST* for you to take is to
- A. suspend all employees immediately if there is no question in your mind as to the validity of the charges
- B. review the personnel records of those involved with the supervisor and make a joint decision on which employees should sustain penalties of loss of annual leave or fines
- C. ask the supervisor to interview each violator and submit written reports to you and thereafter consult with the supervisor about disciplinary actions
- D. deduct three days of annual leave from each employee involved if he pleads guilty in lieu of facing more serious charges

8. Assume that as a manager you must discipline a subordinate, but all of the pertinent facts necessary for a full determination of the appropriate disciplinary action to take are not yet available. However, you fear that a delay in disciplinary action may damage the morale of other employees.
The one of the following which is *MOST* appropriate for you to do in this matter is to
   - A. take immediate disciplinary action as if all the pertinent facts were available
   - B. wait until all the pertinent facts are available before reaching a decision
   - C. inform the subordinate that you know he is guilty, issue a stern warning, and then let him wait for your further action
   - D. reduce the severity of the discipline appropriate for the violation

9. There are two standard dismissal procedures utilized by most public agencies. The first is the "open back door" policy, in which the decision of a supervisor in discharging an employee for reasons of inefficiency cannot be cancelled by the central personnel agency. The second is the "closed back door" policy, in which the central personnel agency can order the supervisor to restore the discharged employee to his position.
Of the following, the *major DISADVANTAGE* of the "closed back door" policy as opposed to the "open back door" policy is that central personnel agencies are
   - A. likely to approve the dismissal of employees when there is inadequate justification
   - B. likely to revoke dismissal actions out of sympathy for employees
   - C. less qualified than employing agencies to evaluate the efficiency of employees
   - D. easily influenced by political, religious, and racial factors

10. The one of the following for which a formal grievance-handling system is *LEAST* useful is in
    - A. reducing the frequency of employee complaints
    - B. diminishing the likelihood of arbitrary action by supervisors
    - C. providing an outlet for employee frustrations

D. bringing employee problems to the attention of higher management
11. The one of the following managers whose leadership style involves the *GREATEST* delegation of authority to subordinates is the one who presents to subordinates
    A. his ideas and invites questions
    B. his decision and persuades them to accept it
    C. the problem, gets their suggestions, and makes his decision
    D. a tentative decision which is subject to change
12. Which of the following is *most likely* to cause employee productivity standards to be set too high?
    A. Standards of productivity are set by first-line supervisors rather than by higher-level managers.
    B. Employees' opinions about productivity standards are sought through written questionnaires.
    C. Initial studies concerning productivity are conducted by staff specialists.
    D. Ideal work conditions assumed in the productivity standards are lacking in actual operations.
13. The one of the following which states the *MAIN* value of an organization chart for a manager is that such charts show the
    A. lines of formal authority
    B. manner in which duties are performed by each employee
    C. flow of work among employees on the same level
    D. specific responsibilities of each position
14. Which of the following *BEST* names the usual role of a line unit with regard to the organization's programs?
    A. Seeking publicity   B. Developing
    C. Carrying out   D. Evaluating
15. Critics of promotion *from within* a public agency argue for hiring *from outside* the agency because they believe that promotion from within leads to
    A. resentment and consequent weakened morale on the part of those not promoted
    B. the perpetuation of outdated practices and policies
    C. a more complex hiring procedure than hiring from outside the agency
    D. problems of objectively appraising someone already in the organization
16. The one of the following management functions which *usually* can be handled *MOST* effectively by a committee is the
    A. settlement of interdepartmental disputes
    B. planning of routine work schedules
    C. dissemination of information
    D. assignment of personnel
17. Assume that you are serving on a committee which is considering proposals in order to recommend a new maintenance policy. After eliminating a number of proposals by unanimous consent, the committee is deadlocked on three proposals. The one of the following which is the *BEST* way for the committee to reach agreement on a proposal they could recommend is to
    A. consider and vote on each proposal separately by secret ballot

9

    B. examine and discuss the three proposals until the proponents of two of them are persuaded they are wrong
    C. reach a synthesis which incorporates the significant features of each proposal
    D. discuss the three proposals until the proponents of each one concede those aspects of the proposals about which there is disagreement
18. A commonly used training and development method for professional staff is the case method, which utilizes the description of a situation, real or simulated, to provide a common base for analysis, discussion, and problem-solving. Of the following, the MOST appropriate time to use the case method is when professional staff needs
    A. insight into their personality problems
    B. practice in applying management concepts to their own problems
    C. practical experience in the assignment of delegated responsibilities
    D. to know how to function in many different capacities
19. The incident process is a training and development method in which trainees are given a very brief statement of an event or of a situation presenting a job incident or an employee problem of special significance.
Of the following, it is MOST appropriate to use the incident process when
    A. trainees need to learn to review and analyze facts before solving a problem
    B. there are a large number of trainees who require the same information
    C. there are too many trainees to carry on effective discussion
    D. trainees are not aware of the effect of their behavior on others
20. The one of the following types of information about which a new clerical employee is usually LEAST concerned during the orientation process is
    A. his specific job duties   B. where he will work
    C. his organization's history D. who his associates will be
21. The one of the following which is the MOST important limitation on the degree to which work should be broken down into specialized tasks is the point at which
    A. there ceases to be sufficient work of a specialized nature to occupy employees
    B. training costs equal the half-yearly savings derived from further specialization
    C. supervision of employees performing specialized tasks becomes more technical than supervision of general employees
    D. it becomes more difficult to replace the specialist than to replace the generalist who performs a complex set of functions
22. When a supervisor is asked for his opinion of the suitability for promotion of a subordinate, the supervisor is actually being asked to predict the subordinate's future behavior in a new role.

Such a prediction is *most likely* to be accurate if the
- A. higher position is similar to the subordinate's current one
- B. higher position requires intangible personal qualities
- C. new position requires a high intellectual level of performance
- D. supervisor has had little personal association with the subordinate away from the job

23. In one form of the non-directive evaluation interview the supervisor communicates his evaluation to the employee and then listens to the employee's response without making further suggestions.
The one of the following which is the PRINCIPAL danger of this method of evaluation is that the employee is most likely to
- A. develop an indifferent attitude towards the supervisor
- B. fail to discover ways of improving his performance
- C. become resistant to change in the organization's structure
- D. place the blame for his shortcomings on his co-workers

24. In establishing rules for his subordinates, a superior should be PRIMARILY concerned with
- A. creating sufficient flexibility to allow for exceptions
- B. making employees aware of the reasons for the rules and the penalties for infractions
- C. establishing the strength of his own position in relation to his subordinates
- D. having his subordinates know that such rules will be imposed in a personal manner

25. The practice of conducting staff training sessions on a periodic basis is *generally* considered
- A. *poor;* it takes employees away from their work assignments
- B. *poor;* all staff training should be done on an individual basis
- C. *good;* it permits the regular introduction of new methods and techniques
- D. *good;* it ensures a high employee productivity rate

KEYS (CORRECT ANSWERS)

TEST 1

1.	C	6.	D	11.	D	16.	C	21.	C
2.	A	7.	B	12.	A	17.	A	22.	D
3.	C	8.	A	13.	C	18.	C	23.	D
4.	B	9.	B	14.	B	19.	A	24.	C
5.	D	10.	D	15.	D	20.	D	25.	C

TEST 2

1.	A	6.	B	11.	C	16.	A	21.	A
2.	A	7.	C	12.	D	17.	C	22.	A
3.	A	8.	B	13.	A	18.	B	23.	B
4.	D	9.	C	14.	C	19.	A	24.	B
5.	C	10.	A	15.	B	20.	C	25.	C

EXAMINATION SECTION
TEST 1

DIRECTIONS: Each question or incomplete statement is followed by several suggested answers or completions. Select the one that BEST answers the question or completes the statement. *PRINT THE LETTER OF THE CORRECT ANSWER IN THE SPACE AT THE RIGHT.*

1. Following are three statements concerning on-the-job training:
    I. On-the-job training is rarely used as a method of training employees.
    II. On-the-job training is often carried on with little or no planning.
    III. On-the-job training is often less expensive than other types.

    Which of the following BEST classifies the above statements into those that are correct and those that are not?

    A. I is correct, but II and III are not
    B. II is correct, but I and III are not
    C. I and II are correct, but III is not
    D. II and III are correct, but I is not

2. The one of the following which is NOT a valid principle for a supervisor to keep in mind when talking to a subordinate about his performance is:

    A. People frequently know when they deserve criticism
    B. Supervisors should be prepared to offer suggestions to subordinates about how to improve their work
    C. Good points should be discussed before bad points
    D. Magnifying a subordinate's faults will get him to improve faster

3. In many organizations information travels quickly through the *grapevine*.
   Following are three statements concerning the *grapevine*:
    I. Information a subordinate does not want to tell her supervisor may reach the supervisor through the *grapevine*.
    II. A supervisor can often do her job better by knowing the information that travels through the *grapevine*.
    III. A supervisor can depend on the *grapevine* as a way to get accurate information from the employees on his staff

    Which one of the following *correctly* classifies the above statements into those which are generally CORRECT and those which are NOT?

    A. II is correct, but I and III are not
    B. III is correct, but I and II are not
    C. I and II are correct, but III is not
    D. I and III are correct, but II is not

4. Following are three statements concerning supervision:
    I. A supervisor knows he is doing a good job if his subordinates depend upon him to make every decision.
    II. A supervisor who delegates authority to his subordinates soon finds that his subordinates begin to resent him.
    III. Giving credit for good work is frequently an effective method of getting subordinates to work harder.

Which one of the following *correctly* classifies the above statements into those that are CORRECT and those that are NOT?

- A. I and II are correct, but III is not
- B. II and III are correct, but I is not
- C. II is correct, but I and III are not
- D. III is correct, but I and II are not

5. Of the following, the LEAST appropriate action for a supervisor to take in preparing a disciplinary case against a subordinate is to

    - A. keep careful records of each incident in which the subordinate has been guilty of misconduct or incompetency, even though immediate disciplinary action may not be necessary
    - B. discuss with the employee each incident of misconduct as it occurs so the employee knows where he stands
    - C. accept memoranda from any other employees who may have been witnesses to acts of misconduct
    - D. keep the subordinate's personnel file confidential so that he is unaware of the evidence being gathered against him

6. Praise by a supervisor can be an important element in motivating subordinates. Following are three statements concerning a supervisor's praise of subordinates:
    - I. In order to be effective, praise must be lavish and constantly restated.
    - II. Praise should be given in a manner which meets the needs of the individual subordinate.
    - III. The subordinate whose work is praised should believe that the praise is earned.

    Which of the following *correctly* classifies the above statements into those that are CORRECT and those that are NOT?

    - A. I is correct, but II and III are not
    - B. II and III are correct, but I is not
    - C. III is correct, but I and II are not
    - D. I and II are correct, but III is not

7. A supervisor feels that he is about to lose his temper while reprimanding a subordinate. Of the following, the BEST action for the supervisor to take is to

    - A. postpone the reprimand for a short time until his self-control is assured
    - B. continue the reprimand because a loss of temper by the supervisor will show the subordinate the seriousness of the error he made
    - C. continue the reprimand because failure to do so will show that the supervisor does not have complete self-control
    - D. postpone the reprimand until the subordinate is capable of understanding the reason for the supervisor's loss of temper

8. Following are three statements concerning various ways of giving orders to subordinates:
   I. An implied order or suggestion is usually appropriate for the inexperienced employee.
   II. A polite request is less likely to upset a sensitive subordinate than a direct order.
   III. A direct order is usually appropriate in an emergency situation.

   Which of the following correctly classifies the above statements into those that are CORRECT and those that are NOT?

   A. I is correct, but II and III are not
   B. II and III are correct, but I is not
   C. III is correct, but I and II are not
   D. I and II are correct, but III is not

9. The one of the following which is NOT an acceptable reason for taking disciplinary action against a subordinate guilty of serious violations of the rules is that

   A. the supervisor can "*let off steam*" against subordinates who break rules frequently
   B. a subordinate whose work continues to be unsatisfactory may be terminated
   C. a subordinate may be encouraged to improve his work
   D. an example is set for other employees

10. At the first meeting with your staff after appointment as a supervisor, you find considerable indifference and some hostility among the participants.
    Of the following, the *most appropriate* way to handle this situation is to

    A. disregard the attitudes displayed and continue to make your presentation until you have completed it
    B. discontinue your presentation but continue the meeting and attempt to find out the reasons for their attitudes
    C. warm up your audience with some good natured statements and anecdotes and then proceed with your presentation
    D. discontinue the meeting and set up personal interviews with the staff members to try to find out the reason for their attitude

11. Use a written rather than oral communication to amend any previous written communication.
    Of the following, the BEST justification for this statement is that

    A. oral changes will be considered more impersonal and thus less important
    B. oral changes will be forgotten or recalled indifferently
    C. written communications are clearer and shorter
    D. written communications are better able to convey feeling tone

4 (#1)

12. Assume that a certain supervisor, when writing important communications to his subordinates, often repeats certain points in different words.
This technique is *generally*

   A. *ineffective;* it tends to confuse rather than help
   B. *effective;* it tends to improve understanding by the subordinates
   C. *ineffective;* it unnecessarily increases the length of the communication and may annoy the subordinates
   D. *effective;* repetition is always an advantage in communications

13. In preparing a letter or a report, a supervisor may wish to persuade the reader of the correctness of some idea or course of action.
The BEST way to accomplish this is for the supervisor to

   A. encourage the reader to make a prompt decision
   B. express each idea in a separate paragraph
   C. present the subject matter of the letter in the first paragraph
   D. state the potential benefits for the reader

14. Effective communications, a basic necessity for successful supervision is a two-way street. A good supervisor needs to listen to, as well as disseminate, information and he must be able to encourage his subordinates to communicate with him. Which of the following suggestions will contribute LEAST to improving the *listening power* of a supervisor?

   A. Don't assume anything; don't anticipate, and don't let a subordinate think you know what he is going to say
   B. Don't interupt; let him have his full say even if it requires a second session that day to get the full story
   C. React quickly to his statements so that he knows you are interested, even if you must draw some conclusions prematurely
   D. Try to understand the real need for his talking to you even if it is quite different from the subject under discussion

15. Of the following, the MOST useful approach for the supervisor to take toward the informal employee communications network know as the *grapevine* is to

   A. remain isolated from it, but not take any active steps to eliminate it
   B. listen to it, but not depend on it for accurate information
   C. use it to disseminate confidential information
   D. eliminate it as diplomatically as possible

16. If a supervisor is asked to estimate the number of employees that he believes he will need in his unit in the coming fiscal year, the supervisor should FIRST attempt to learn the

   A. nature and size of the workload his unit will have during that time
   B. cost of hiring and training new employees
   C. average number of employee absences per year
   D. number of employees needed to indirectly support or assist his unit

17. An important supervisory responsibility is coordinating the operations of the unit. This may include setting work schedules, controlling work quality, establishing interim due dates, etc. In order to handle this task it has been divided into the following five stages:
    I. Determine the steps or sequence required for the tasks to be performed.
    II. Give the orders, either written or oral, to begin work on the Tasks.
    III. check up by following each task to make sure it is proceeding according to plan.
    IV. Schedule the jobs by setting a time for each task of operation to begin and end.
    V. Control the process by correcting conditions which interfere with the plan.

    The MOST logical sequence in which these planning steps should be performed is

    A. I, II, III, IV, V
    B. II, I, V, III, IV
    C. I, IV, II, III, V
    D. IV, I, II, III, V

18. Assume that a supervisor calls a meeting with the staff under his supervision in order to discuss several proposals. After some discussion, he realizes that he strongly disagrees with one proposal that four of the staff have rather firmly favored.
    At this point, he could BEST handle the situation by saying

    A. *I have the responsibility for this decision, and I must disagree.*
    B. *I am just reminding you that I have had a great deal more experience in these matters.*
    C. *You have presented some good points, but perhaps we could look at it another way.*
    D. *The only way that this proposal can be disposed of is to defer it for further discussion.*

19. As far as the social activities and groups of his subordinates are concerned, a supervisor in a large organization can BEST strengthen his tools of leadership by

    A. emphasizing the organization as a whole and forbidding the formation of groups
    B. ignoring the groups as much as possible and dealing with each subordinate as an individual
    C. learning about the status structure of employee groups and their values
    D. avoiding any relationship with groups

20. If a subordinate asks you, his supervisor, for advice in planning his career in the department you *should*

    A. encourage him to feel that he can easily reach the top of his occupational ladder
    B. discourage him from setting his hopes too high
    C. discuss career opportunities realistically with him
    D. explain that you have no control over his opportunities for advancement

21. A supervisor's evaluation of an employee is usually based upon a combination of objective facts and subjective judgments or opinions.
    Which of the following aspects of an employee's work or performance is *most likely* to be subjectively evaluated?

    A. Quantity
    B. Accuracy
    C. Attitude
    D. Attendance

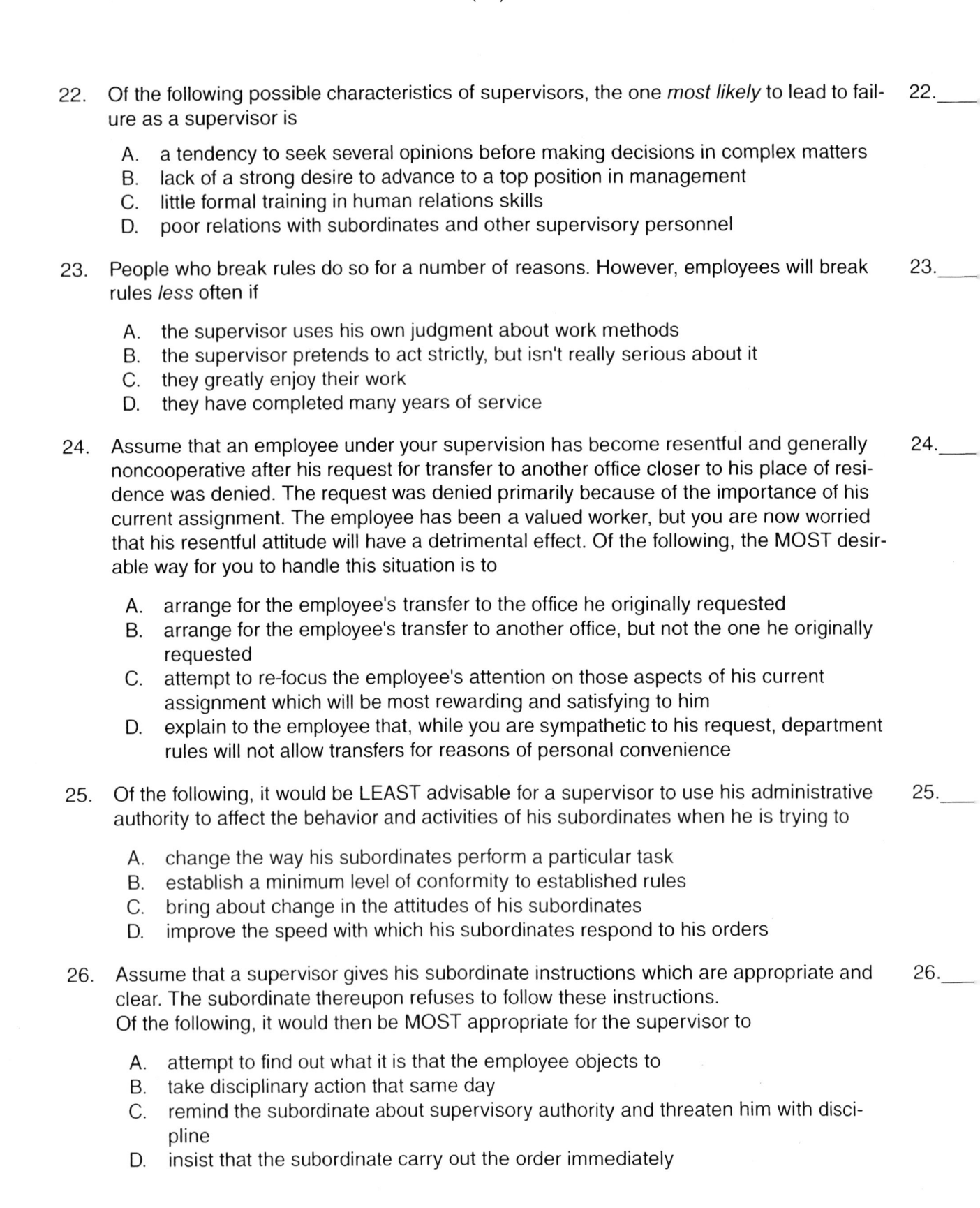

22. Of the following possible characteristics of supervisors, the one *most likely* to lead to failure as a supervisor is

    A. a tendency to seek several opinions before making decisions in complex matters
    B. lack of a strong desire to advance to a top position in management
    C. little formal training in human relations skills
    D. poor relations with subordinates and other supervisory personnel

23. People who break rules do so for a number of reasons. However, employees will break rules *less* often if

    A. the supervisor uses his own judgment about work methods
    B. the supervisor pretends to act strictly, but isn't really serious about it
    C. they greatly enjoy their work
    D. they have completed many years of service

24. Assume that an employee under your supervision has become resentful and generally noncooperative after his request for transfer to another office closer to his place of residence was denied. The request was denied primarily because of the importance of his current assignment. The employee has been a valued worker, but you are now worried that his resentful attitude will have a detrimental effect. Of the following, the MOST desirable way for you to handle this situation is to

    A. arrange for the employee's transfer to the office he originally requested
    B. arrange for the employee's transfer to another office, but not the one he originally requested
    C. attempt to re-focus the employee's attention on those aspects of his current assignment which will be most rewarding and satisfying to him
    D. explain to the employee that, while you are sympathetic to his request, department rules will not allow transfers for reasons of personal convenience

25. Of the following, it would be LEAST advisable for a supervisor to use his administrative authority to affect the behavior and activities of his subordinates when he is trying to

    A. change the way his subordinates perform a particular task
    B. establish a minimum level of conformity to established rules
    C. bring about change in the attitudes of his subordinates
    D. improve the speed with which his subordinates respond to his orders

26. Assume that a supervisor gives his subordinate instructions which are appropriate and clear. The subordinate thereupon refuses to follow these instructions.
    Of the following, it would then be MOST appropriate for the supervisor to

    A. attempt to find out what it is that the employee objects to
    B. take disciplinary action that same day
    C. remind the subordinate about supervisory authority and threaten him with discipline
    D. insist that the subordinate carry out the order immediately

27. Of the following, the MOST effective way to identify training needs resulting from gradual changes in procedure is to

    A. monitor on a continuous basis the actual jobs performed and the skills required
    B. periodically send out a written questionnaire asking personnel to identify their needs
    C. conduct interviews at regular intervals with selected employees
    D. consult employees' personnel records

28. Assume that you, as a supervisor, have had a new employee assigned to you. If the duties of his position can be broken into independent parts, which of the following is usually the BEST way to train this new employee?
Start with

    A. the easiest duties and progressively proceed to the most difficult
    B. something easy; move to something difficult; then back to something easy
    C. something difficult; move to something easy; then to something difficult
    D. the most difficult duties and progressively proceed to the easiest

29. The oldest and most commonly used training technique is on-the-job training. Instruction is given to the worker by his supervisor or by another employee. Such training is essential in most jobs, although it is not always effective when used alone.
This technique, however, *can* be effectively used alone if

    A. the skills involved can be learned quickly
    B. a large number of people are to be trained at one time
    C. other forms of training have not been previously used with the people involved
    D. the skills to be taught are mental rather than manual

30. It is generally agreed that the learning process is facilitated in proportion to the amount of feedback that the learner is given about his performance.
Following are three statements concerning the learning process:
    I. The more specific the learner's knowledge of how he performed, the more rapid his improvement and the higher his level of performance.
    II. Giving the learner knowledge of his results does not affect his motivation to learn.
    III. Learners who are not given feedback will set up subjective criteria and evaluate their own performance.
Which of the following choices lists ALL of the above statements that are *generally* correct?

    A. I and II *only*   B. I and III *only*
    C. II and III *only*   D. I, II and III

KEY (CORRECT ANSWERS)

1.	D	11.	B	21.	C
2.	D	12.	B	22.	D
3.	C	13.	D	23.	C
4.	D	14.	C	24.	C
5.	D	15.	B	25.	C
6.	B	16.	A	26.	A
7.	A	17.	C	27.	A
8.	B	18.	C	28.	A
9.	A	19.	C	29.	A
10.	D	20.	C	30.	B

TEST 2

DIRECTIONS: Each question or incomplete statement is followed by several suggested answers or completions. Select the one that BEST answers the question or completes the statement. *PRINT THE LETTER OF THE CORRECT ANSWER IN THE SPACE AT THE RIGHT.*

Questions 1–6.

DIRECTIONS: Questions 1 through 6 are to be answered SOLELY on the basis of the information given in the following paragraph.

The use of role-playing as a training technique was developed during the past decade by social scientists, particularly psychologists, who have been active in training experiments. Originally, this technique was applied by clinical psychologists who discovered that a patient appears to gain understanding of an emotionally disturbing situation when encouraged to act out roles in that situation. As applied in government and business organizations, the purpose of role-playing is to aid employees to understand certain work problems involving interpersonal relations and to enable observers to evaluate various reactions to them. Thus, for example, on the problem of handling grievances, two individuals from the group might be selected to act out extemporaneously the parts of subordinate and supervisor. When this situation is enacted by various pairs among the class and the techniques and results are discussed, the members of the group are presumed to reach conclusions about the most effective means of handling similar situations. Often the use of role reversal, where participants take parts different from their actual work roles, assists individuals to gain more insight into other people's problems and viewpoints. Although role-playing can be a rewarding training device, the trainer must be aware of his responsibilities. If this technique is to be successful, thorough briefing of both actors and observers as to the situation in question, the participants' roles, and what to look for, is essential.

1. The role-playing technique was FIRST used for the purpose of

    A. measuring the effectiveness of training programs
    B. training supervisors in business organizations
    C. treating emotionally disturbed patients
    D. handling employee grievances

2. When role-playing is used in private business as a training device, the CHIEF aim is to

    A. develop better relations between supervisor and subordinate in the handling of grievances
    B. come up with a solution to a specific problem that has arisen
    C. determine the training needs of the group
    D. increase employee understanding of the human relation factors in work situations

3. From the above passage, it is MOST reasonable to conclude that when role-playing is used, it is preferable to have the roles acted out by

    A. only one set of actors
    B. no more than two sets of actors
    C. several different sets of actors
    D. the trainer or trainers of the group

4. Based on the above passage, a trainer using the technique of role reversal in a problem of first-line supervision should assign a senior employee to play the part of a(n)

   A. new employee
   B. senior employee
   C. principal employee
   D. angry citizen

5. It can be inferred from the above passage that a limitation of role-play as a training method is that

   A. many work situations do not lend themselves to role-play
   B. employees are not experienced enough as actors to play the roles realistically
   C. only trainers who have psychological training can use it successfully
   D. participants who are observing and not acting do not benefit from it

6. To obtain good results from the use of role-play in training, a trainer should give participants

   A. a minimum of information about the situation so that they can act spontaneously
   B. scripts which illustrate the best method for handling the situation
   C. a complete explanation of the problem and the roles to be acted out
   D. a summary of work problems which involve interpersonal relations

7. Of the following, the MOST important reason for a supervisor to prepare good written reports is that

   A. a supervisor is rated on the quality of his reports
   B. decisions are often made on the basis of the reports
   C. such reports take less time for superiors to review
   D. such reports demonstrate efficiency of department operations

8. Of the following, the BEST test of a good report is whether it

   A. provides the information needed
   B. shows the good sense of the writer
   C. is prepared according to a proper format
   D. is grammatical and neat

9. When a supervisor writes a report, he can BEST show that he has an understanding of the subject of the report by

   A. including necessary facts and omitting non-essential details
   B. using statistical data
   C. giving his conclusions but not the data on which they are based
   D. using a technical vocabulary

10. Suppose you and another supervisor on the same level are assigned to work together on a report. You disagree strongly with one of the recommendations the other supervisor wants to include in the report but you cannot change his views.
    Of the following, it would be BEST that

    A. you refuse to accept responsibility for the report
    B. you ask that someone else be assigned to this project to replace you
    C. each of you state his own ideas about this recommendation in the report
    D. you give in to the other supervisor's opinion for the sake of harmony

11. Standardized forms are often provided for submitting reports.
Of the following, the MOST important advantage of using standardized forms for reports is that

11.____

   A. they take less time to prepare than individually written reports
   B. necessary information is less likely to be omitted
   C. the responsibility for preparing these reports can be delegated to subordinates
   D. the person making the report can omit information he considers unimportant

12. A report which may BEST be classed as a *periodic* report is one which

12.____

   A. requires the same type of information at regular intervals
   B. contains detailed information which is to be retained in permanent records
   C. is prepared whenever a special situation occurs
   D. lists information in graphic form

13. Which one of the following is NOT an important reason for keeping accurate records in an office?

13.____

   A. Facts will be on hand when decisions have to be made.
   B. The basis for past actions can be determined.
   C. Information needed by other bureaus can be furnished.
   D. Filing is easier when records are properly made out.

14. Suppose you are preparing to write a report recommending a change in a certain procedure. You learn that another supervisor made a report a few years ago suggesting a change in this same procedure, but that no action was taken.
Of the following, it would be MOST desirable for you to

14.____

   A. avoid reading the other supervisor's report so that you will write with a more up-to-date point of view
   B. make no recommendation since management seems to be against any change in the procedure
   C. read the other report before you write your report to see what bearing it may have on your recommendations
   D. avoid including in your report any information that can be obtained by referring to the other report

15. If a report you are preparing to your superior is going to be a very long one, it would be DESIRABLE to include a summary of your basic conclusions

15.____

   A. at the end of the report
   B. at the beginning of the report
   C. in a separate memorandum
   D. right after you present the supporting data

16. Suppose that some bureau and department policies must be very frequently applied by your subordinates while others rarely come into use.
    As a supervising employee, a GOOD technique for you to use in fulfilling your responsibility of seeing to it that policies are adhered to is to

    A. ask the director of the bureau to issue to all employees an explanation in writing of all policies
    B. review with your subordinates every week those policies which have daily application
    C. follow up on and explain at regular intervals the application of those policies which are not used very often by your subordinates
    D. recommend to your superiors that policies rarely used be changed or dropped

17. The BASIC purpose behind the principle of delegation of authority is to

    A. give the supervisor who is delegating a chance to acquire skills in higher level functions
    B. free the supervisor from routine tasks in order that he may do the important parts of his job
    C. prevent supervisors from overstepping the lines of authority which have been established
    D. place the work delegated in the hands of those employees who can perform it best

18. A district commander can BEST assist management in long-range planning by

    A. reporting to his superiors any changing conditions in the district
    B. maintaining a neat and efficiently run office
    C. scheduling work so that areas with a high rate of non-compliance get more intensive coverage
    D. properly training new personnel assigned to his district

19. Suppose that new quarters have been rented for your district office.
    Of the following, the LEAST important factor to be considered in planning the layout of the office is the

    A. need for screening confidential activities from unauthorized persons
    B. relative importance of the various types of work
    C. areas of noise concentration
    D. convenience with which communication between sections of the office can be achieved

20. Of the following, the MOST basic effect of organizing a department so that lines of authority are clearly defined and duties are specifically assigned is to

    A. increase the need for close supervision
    B. decrease the initiative of subordinates
    C. lessen the possibility of duplication of work
    D. increase the responsibilities of supervisory personnel

21. An accepted management principle is that decisions should be delegated to the lowest point in the organization at which they can be made effectively.
The one of the following which is MOST likely to be a result of the application of this principle is that

   A. no factors will be overlooked in making decisions
   B. prompt action will follow the making of decisions
   C. decisions will be made more rapidly
   D. coordination of decisions that are made will be simplified

22. Suppose you are a supervisor and need some guidance from a higher authority.
In which one of the following situations would it be PERMISSIBLE for you to bypass the regular upward channels of communication in the chain of command?

   A. In an emergency when your superior is not available
   B. When it is not essential to get a quick reply
   C. When you feel your immediate superior is not understanding of the situation
   D. When you want to obtain information that you think your superior does not have

23. Of the following, the CHIEF limitation of the organization chart as it is generally used in business and government is that the chart

   A. makes lines of responsibility and authority undesirably definite and formal
   B. is often out of date as soon as it is completed
   C. does not show human factors and informal working relationships
   D. is usually too complicated

24. The *span of control* for any supervisor is the

   A. number of tasks he is expected to perform himself
   B. amount of office space he and his subordinates occupy
   C. amount of work he is responsible for getting out
   D. number of subordinates he can supervise effectively

25. Of the following duties performed by a supervising employee, which would be considered a LINE function rather than a staff function?

   A. Evaluation of office personnel
   B. Recommendations for disciplinary action
   C. Initiating budget requests for replacement of equipment
   D. Inspections, at irregular times, of conditions and staff in the field

KEY (CORRECT ANSWERS)

1.	C		11.	B
2.	D		12.	A
3.	C		13.	D
4.	A		14.	C
5.	A		15.	B
6.	C		16.	C
7.	B		17.	B
8.	A		18.	A
9.	A		19.	B
10.	C		20.	C

21. B
22. A
23. C
24. D
25. D

PREPARING WRITTEN MATERIAL

PARAGRAPH REARRANGEMENT
COMMENTARY

The sentences which follow are in scrambled order. You are to rearrange them in proper order and indicate the letter choice containing the correct answer at the space at the right.

Each group of sentences in this section is actually a paragraph presented in scrambled order. Each sentence in the group has a place in that paragraph; no sentence is to be left out. You are to read each group of sentences and decide upon the best order in which to put the sentences so as to form as well-organized paragraph.

The questions in this section measure the ability to solve a problem when all the facts relevant to its solution are not given.

More specifically, certain positions of responsibility and authority require the employee to discover connections between events sometimes, apparently, unrelated. In order to do this, the employee will find it necessary to correctly infer that unspecified events have probably occurred or are likely to occur. This ability becomes especially important when action must be taken on incomplete information.

Accordingly, these questions require competitors to choose among several suggested alternatives, each of which presents a different sequential arrangement of the events. Competitors must choose the MOST logical of the suggested sequences.

In order to do so, they may be required to draw on general knowledge to infer missing concepts or events that are essential to sequencing the given events. Competitors should be careful to infer only what is essential to the sequence. The plausibility of the wrong alternatives will always require the inclusion of unlikely events or of additional chains of events which are NOT essential to sequencing the given events.

It's very important to remember that you are looking for the best of the four possible choices, and that the best choice of all may not even be one of the answers you're given to choose from.

There is no one right way to these problems. Many people have found it helpful to first write out the order of the sentences, as they would have arranged them, on their scrap paper before looking at the possible answers. If their optimum answer is there, this can save them some time. If it isn't, this method can still give insight into solving the problem. Others find it most helpful to just go through each of the possible choices, contrasting each as they go along. You should use whatever method feels comfortable, and works, for you.

While most of these types of questions are not that difficult, we've added a higher percentage of the difficult type, just to give you more practice. Usually there are only one or two questions on this section that contain such subtle distinctions that you're unable to answer confidently, and you then may find yourself stuck deciding between two possible choices, neither of which you're sure about.

EXAMINATION SECTION
TEST 1

DIRECTIONS: The sentences that follow are in scrambled order. You are to rearrange them in proper order and indicate the letter choice containing the CORRECT answer. *PRINT THE LETTER OF THE CORRECT ANSWER IN THE SPACE AT THE RIGHT.*

1. Fire Marshal Adams has arrested a man for pulling a false alarm. He has recorded the following items of information about the incident in his notebook for use in his subsequent report:
    I. I was on surveillance at a frequently pulled false alarm box located at Edison Street and Harvard Road.
    II. At 1605 hours, I observed the white male, with long brown hair and a mustache, wearing black pants and a red shirt, pull the fire alarm box.
    III. I interviewed the officer of the first due ladder company, Lt. Morgan - L-37, who informed me that a search of the area disclosed no cause for an alarm to be transmitted.
    IV. A man wearing a red shirt, black pants, with long brown hair and a mustache came out of Ryan's Pub, located at Edison Street and Harvard Road, and walked directly to the alarm box.
    V. I stopped the man about five blocks away at 33rd Street and Harvard Road and asked him why he pulled the fire alarm box, and he replied, *Because I felt like it.*

    The MOST logical order for the above sentences to appear in the report is

    A. I, IV, II, III, V
    B. I, II, III, IV, V
    C. I, IV, III, II, V
    D. I, IV, V, II, III

    1.____

2. A fire marshal is preparing a report regarding Tom Jones, who was a witness to an arson fire at his apartment building. Following are five sentences which will be included in the report:
    I. On July 16, I responded to the fire building, address 2020 Elm Street, to interview Tom Jones.
    II. Tom Jones described the *super* (name unknown) as a middle-aged male with beard, six feet tall, wearing a blue jumpsuit.
    III. Tom Jones stated that he saw the *super* of the building next door set the fire.
    IV. After being advised of his constitutional rights at the 44th Precinct detective's squad room, the *super* confessed.
    V. I interviewed the *super* and took him to the precinct for further investigation.

    The MOST logical order for the above sentences to appear in the report is

    A. I, II, III, V, IV
    B. I, II, III, IV, V
    C. I, III, II, IV, V
    D. I, III, II, V, IV

    2.____

3. A fire marshal is preparing a report on a shooting incident which will include the following five sentences:
   I. I ran around the corner and observed a man pointing a gun at another man.
   II. I informed the man I was a police officer and that he should drop his gun.
   III. I was on the corner of 4th Avenue and 43rd Street when I heard a gunshot coming from around the corner.
   IV. The man turned around and pointed his gun at me.
   V. I fired once, shooting him in the chest and causing him to fall to the ground.
   The MOST logical order for the above sentences to appear in the report is

   A. I, III, IV, II, V   B. IV, V, II, I, III
   C. III, I, II, IV, V   D. III, I, V, II, IV

4. Fire Marshal Smith is writing a report. The report will include the following five sentences:
   I. I asked the woman for a description of the man and his location in the building.
   II. When I said, *Don't move, Five Marshal,* the man dropped the can containing a flammable liquid.
   III. I transmitted on my handie-talkie for fire companies to respond.
   IV. A woman approached our car and said there was a man pouring a liquid, which she thought to be gasoline, on a staircase at 123 East Street.
   V. Upon entering that location, I observed a man spilling a liquid on the floor.
   The MOST logical order for the above sentences to appear on the interview sheet is

   A. IV, I, V, II, III   B. I, IV, III, V, II
   C. V, II, IV, I, III   D. IV, III, I, V, II

5. Fire Marshal Fox is completing an interview report for a fire in the kitchen of an apartment at 1700 Clayton Road. The following five sentences will be included in the interview report:
   I. This is the first fire in which Mrs. Brown has ever been involved.
   II. A neighbor smelled the food burning and called the Fire Department.
   III. Mrs. Brown has been a tenant in Apt. 4C for 7 years.
   IV. Mrs. Brown was very tired and laid down to rest and fell asleep.
   V. Mrs. Brown was cooking beef stew in the kitchen after coming home from work.
   The MOST logical order for the above sentences to appear in the report is

   A. II, III, I, IV, V   B. III, V, IV, II, I
   C. I, III, II, V, IV   D. III, V, I, IV, II

6. A fire marshal is completing a report of an arson fire. The report will contain the following five statements made by a witness:
   I. I heard the sound of breaking glass; and when I looked out my window, I saw orange flames coming from the building across the street.
   II. I saw two young men on bicycles rapidly riding away, one with long blond hair, the other had long brown hair.
   III. He made a threat to get even when he was being evicted.
   IV. The young man with long blond hair was evicted from the fire building last week.
   V. The two young men rode in the direction of Flowers Avenue.
   The MOST logical order for the above statements to appear in the report is

A. I, II, V, IV, III	B. I, II, IV, V, III
C. III, I, V, II, IV	D. III, I, II, IV, V

7. A fire marshal is preparing a report regarding an eleven-year-old who was burned in a fire at the Midtown School for Boys. The report will include the following five sentences:
   I. The child described the fire-setter as a male with glasses, five feet tall, wearing a blue uniform.
   II. On December 12, I responded to Hill Top Hospital to interview a child who was burned in a fire at the Midtown School for Boys.
   III. The male perpetrator made a full confession in front of the Assistant District Attorney at the precinct.
   IV. I responded to the school, after interviewing the boy, and found a security guard who fit the description.
   V. I interviewed the security guard and took him to the precinct for further questioning.

   The MOST logical order for the above sentences to appear in the fire report is

A. I, IV, V, II, III	B. IV, III, II, I, V
C. II, I, IV, V, III	D. II, IV, I, V, III

8. A fire marshal is preparing a report concerning a fire in an auto body shop. The report will contain the following five sentences:
   I. The shop owner stated that he argued with a customer about the cost of a repair job.
   II. The shop owner will be the complainant in the arson case.
   III. While on surveillance, my partner and I saw the fire and called it in over the Department radio.
   IV. The customer paid the bill and left saying, *I'll fix you for charging so much.*
   V. According to witnesses, the customer returned to the shop and threw a Molotov cocktail on the floor.

   The MOST logical order for the above sentences to appear in the report is

A. I, IV, V, II, III	B. III, I, IV, V, II
C. V, I, IV, III, II	D. III, V, I, IV, II

9. Security Officer Mace is completing an entry in her memo-book. The entry has the following five sentences:
   I. I observed the defendant removing a radio from a facility vehicle.
   II. I placed the defendant under arrest and escorted him to the patrolroom.
   III. I was patrolling the facility parking lot.
   IV. I asked the defendant to show identification. V. I determined that the defendant was not authorized to remove the radio.

   The MOST logical order for these sentences to be entered in Officer Mace's memo-book is

A. I, III, II, IV, V	B. II, V, IV, I, III
C. III, I, IV, V, II	D. IV, V, II, I, III

10. Security Officer Riley is completing an entry in his memo-book. The entry has the following five sentences:
    I. Anna Jones admitted that she stole Mary Green's wallet.
    II. I approached the women and asked them who they were and why they were arguing.
    III. I arrested Anna Jones for stealing Mary Green's wallet.
    IV. They identified themselves and Mary Green accused Anna Jones of stealing her wallet.
    V. I was in the lobby area when I observed two women arguing about a wallet.
    The MOST logical order for these sentences to be entered in Officer Riley's memo-book is

    A. II, IV, I, III, V
    B. III, I, IV, V, II
    C. IV, I, V, II, III
    D. V, II, IV, I, III

11. Assume that Security Officer John Ryan is completing an entry in his memobook. The entry has the following five sentences:
    I. I then cleared the immediate area of visitors and staff.
    II. I noticed smoke coming from a broom closet outside Room A71.
    III. Sergeant Mueller arrived with other officers to assist in clearing the area.
    IV. Upon investigation, I determined the smoke was due to burning material in the broom closet.
    V. I pulled the corridor fire alarm and notified Sergeant Mueller of the fire.
    The MOST logical order for these sentences to be entered in Officer Ryan's memo-book is

    A. II, III, IV, V, I
    B. II, IV, V, I, III
    C. IV, I, II, III, V
    D. V, III, II, I, IV

12. Security Officer Hernandez is completing an entry in his memobook. The entry has the following five sentences:
    I. I asked him to leave the premises immediately.
    II. A visitor complained that there was a strange man loitering in Clinic B hallway.
    III. I went to investigate and saw a man dressed in rags sitting on the floor of the hallway.
    IV. As he walked out, he started yelling that he had no place to go.
    V. I asked to see identification, but he said that he did not have any.
    The MOST logical order for these sentences to be entered in Officer Hernandez's memobook is

    A. II, III, V, I, IV
    B. III, I, II, IV, V
    C. IV, I, V, II, III
    D. III, I, V, II, IV

13. Officer Hogan is completing an entry in his memobook. The entry has the following five sentences:
    I. When the fighting had stopped, I transmitted a message requesting medical assistance for Mr. Perkins.
    II. Special Officer Manning assisted me in stopping the fight,
    III. When I arrived at the scene, I saw a client, Adam Finley, strike a facility employee, Peter Perkins.
    IV. As I attempted to break up the fight, Special Officer Manning came on the scene.
    V. I received a radio message from Sergeant Valez to investigate a possible fight in progress in the waiting room.

    The MOST logical order for these sentences to be entered in Officer Hogan's memo-book is

    A. II, I, IV, V, III
    B. III, V, II, IV, I
    C. IV, V, III, I, II
    D. V, III, IV, II, I

14. Police Officer White is preparing a crime report concerning the burglary of Mr. Smith's home. The report will contain the following five sentences:
    I. Upon entering the house, Mr. Smith noticed that the mortgage money, which had been left on the kitchen table, had been taken.
    II. An investigation by the reporting Officer determined that the burglar had left the house through the first floor rear door.
    III. Further investigation revealed that there were no witnesses to the burglary.
    IV. In addition, several pieces of jewelry were missing from a first floor bedroom.
    V. After arriving at home, Mr. Smith discovered that someone had broken into the house by jimmying the front door.

    The MOST logical order for the above sentences to appear in the report is

    A. V, IV, II, III, I
    B. V, I, III, IV, II
    C. V, I, IV, II, III
    D. V, IV, II, I, III

15. Police Officer Jenner responds to the scene of a burglary at 2106 La Vista Boulevard. He is approached by an elderly man named Richard Jenkins, whose account of the incident includes the following five sentences:
    I. I saw that the lock on my apartment door had been smashed and the door was open.
    II. My apartment was a shambles; my belongings were everywhere and my television set was missing.
    III. As I walked down the hallway toward the bedroom, I heard someone opening a window.
    IV. I left work at 5:30 P.M. and took the bus home.
    V. At that time, I called the police.

    The MOST logical order for the above sentences to appear in the report is

    A. I, V, IV, II, III
    B. IV, I, II, III, V
    C. I, V, II, III, IV
    D. IV, III, II, V, I

16. Police Officer LaJolla is writing an Incident Report in which back-up assistance was required. The report will contain the following five sentences:
   I. The radio dispatcher asked what my location was and he then dispatched patrol cars for back-up assistance.
   II. At approximately 9:30 P.M., while I was walking my assigned footpost, a gunman fired three shots at me.
   III. I quickly turned around and saw a White male, approximately 5'10", with black hair, wearing blue jeans, a yellow T-shirt, and white sneakers, running across the avenue carrying a handgun.
   IV. When the back-up officers arrived, we searched the area but could not find the suspect.
   V. I advised the radio dispatcher that a gunman had just fired a gun at me, and then I gave the dispatcher a description of the man.

   The MOST logical order for the above sentences to appear in the report is

   A. III, V, II, IV, I
   B. II, III, V, I, IV
   C. III, II, IV, I, V
   D. II, V, I, III, IV

17. Police Officer Engle is completing a Complaint Report of a burglary which occurred at Monty's Bar. The following five sentences will be included in the Complaint Report:
   I. The owner said that approximately $600 was taken, along with eight bottles of expensive brandy.
   II. The burglar apparently gained entry to the bar through the window and exited through the front door.
   III. When Mr. Barrett returned to reopen the bar at 1:00 P.M., he found the front door open and items thrown all over the bar.
   IV. Mr. Barrett, the owner of Monty's Bar, said he closed the bar at 4:00 M. and locked all the doors.
   V. After interviewing the owner, I conducted a search of the bar and found that a window in the back of the bar was broken.

   The MOST logical order for the above sentences to appear in the report is

   A. II, IV, III, V, I
   B. IV, III, I, V, II
   C. IV, II, III, I, V
   D. II, V, IV, III, I

18. Police Officer Revson is writing a report concerning a vehicle pursuit. His report will include the following five sentences:
   I. I followed the vehicle for several blocks and then motioned to the driver to pull the car over to the curb and stop.
   II. I informed the radio dispatcher that I was in a high-speed pursuit.
   III. When the driver ignored me, I turned on my siren and the driver increased his speed.
   IV. The vehicle hit a tree, and I was able to arrest the driver.
   V. While on patrol in Car #4135, I observed a motorist driving suspiciously.

   The MOST logical order for the above sentences to appear in the report is

   A. V, I, III, II, IV
   B. II, V, III, I, IV
   C. V, I, II, IV, III
   D. II, I, V, IV, III

7 (#1)

19. Crime Reports are completed by Police Officers. One section of a report contains the following five sentences:
    I. The man, seeing that the woman had the watch, pushed Mr. Lugano to the ground.
    II. Frank Lugano was walking into the Flame Diner on Queens Boulevard when he was jostled by a man in front of him.
    III. A few minutes later, Mr. Lugano told a police officer on foot patrol about a man and a woman taking his watch.
    IV. As soon as he was jostled, a woman reached toward Mr. Lugano's wrist and removed his expensive watch.
    V. The man and woman, after taking Mr. Lugano's watch, ran around the corner.

    The MOST logical order for the above sentences to appear in the report is

    A. II, IV, I, III, V
    B. II, IV, I, V, III
    C. IV, I, III, II, V
    D. IV, II, I, V, III

20. Detective Adams completed a Crime Report which includes the following five sentences:
    I. I arrived at the scene of the crime at 10:20 A.M. and began to question Mr. Sands about the security devices he had installed.
    II. Several clearly identifiable fingerprints were found.
    III. A Fingerprint Unit specialist arrived at the scene and immediately began to dust for fingerprints.
    IV. After questioning Mr. Sands, I called the Fingerprint Unit.
    V. On Friday morning at 10 A.M., Mr. Sands, the owner of the High Fashion Fur Store on Fifth Avenue, called the precinct to report that his safe had been broken into.

    The MOST logical order for the above sentences to appear in the Crime Report is

    A. I, V, IV, III, II
    B. I, V, III, IV, II
    C. V, I, IV, II, III
    D. V, I, IV, III, II

KEY (CORRECT ANSWERS)

1. A	11. B
2. D	12. A
3. C	13. D
4. A	14. C
5. B	15. B
6. A	16. B
7. C	17. B
8. B	18. A
9. C	19. B
10. D	20. D

TEST 2

DIRECTIONS: The sentences that follow are in scrambled order. You are to rearrange them in proper order and indicate the letter choice containing the CORRECT answer. *PRINT THE LETTER OF THE CORRECT ANSWER IN THE SPACE AT THE RIGHT.*

1. Police Officer Ling is preparing a Complaint Report of a missing person. His report will contain the following five sentences:

    I. I was greeted by Mrs. Miah Ali, who stated her daughter Lisa, age 17, did not return from school.
    II. I questioned Mrs. Ali as to what time her daughter left for school and what type of clothing she was wearing.
    III. I notified the Patrol Sergeant, searched the building and area, and prepared a Missing Person Complaint Report.
    IV. I received a call from the radio dispatcher to respond to 9 Maple Street, Apartment 1H, on a missing person complaint.
    V. Mrs. Ali informed me that Lisa was wearing a grey suit and black shoes, and departed for school at 7:30 A.M.

    The MOST logical order for the above sentences to appear in the report is

    A. IV, I, V, II, III
    B. I, IV, V, III, II
    C. IV, I, II, V, III
    D. III, I, IV, II, V

1.____

2. Police Officer Dunn is preparing a Complaint Report which will include the following five sentences:

    I. Mrs. Field screamed and fought with the man.
    II. A man wearing a blue ski mask grabbed Mrs. Field's purse.
    III. Mrs. Field was shopping on 34th Street and Broadway at 1 o'clock in the afternoon.
    IV. The man then ran around the corner.
    V. The man was white, five feet six inches tall with a medium build.

    The MOST logical order for the above sentences to appear in the report is

    A. I, V, II, IV, III
    B. III, II, I, IV, V
    C. III, IV, V, I, II
    D. V, IV, III, I, II

2.____

3. Police Officer Davis is preparing a written report concerning child abuse. The report will include the following five sentences:

    I. I responded to the scene and was met by an adult and a child who was approximately four years old.
    II. I was notified by an unidentified pedestrian of a possible case of child abuse at 325 Belair Terrace.
    III. The adult told me that the child fell and that the police were not needed.
    IV. I felt that this might be a case of child abuse, and I requested that a Sergeant respond to the scene.
    V. The child was bleeding from the head and had several bruises on the face.

    The MOST logical order for the above sentences to appear in the report is

    A. II, I, V, III, IV
    B. I, II, IV, III, V
    C. I, III, IV, II, V
    D. II, IV, I, V, III

3.____

4. The following five sentences will be part of a memobook entry concerning found property:

    I. Mr. Gustav said that while cleaning the lobby he found six credit cards and a passport.
    II. The credit cards and passport were issued to Manuel Gomez.
    III. I went to the precinct to give the property to the Desk Officer.
    IV. I prepared a receipt listing the property, gave the receipt to Mr. Gustav, and had him sign my memobook.
    V. While on foot patrol, I was approached by Mr. Gustav, the superintendent of 50-12 Maiden Parkway.

The MOST logical order for the above sentences to appear in the memobook is

A. V, I, II, IV, III
B. I, II, IV, III, V
C. V, I, III, IV, II
D. I, IV, III, II, V

5. Police Officer Thomas is making a memobook entry that will include the following five sentences:

    I. My partner obtained a brief description of the suspects and the direction they were heading when they left the store.
    II. Edward Lemkin was asked to come with us to search the immediate area.
    III. I transmitted this information over the radio.
    IV. At the corner of 72nd Street and Broadway, our patrol car was stopped by Edward Lemkin, the owner of PJ Records.
    V. He told us that a group of teenagers stole some merchandise from his record store.

The MOST logical order for the above sentences to appear in the report is

A. V, IV, I, III, II
B. IV, V, I, III, II
C. V, I, III, II, IV
D. IV, I, III, II, V

6. Police Officer Caldwell is completing a Complaint Report. The report will include the following five sentences:

    I. When I yelled, *Don't move, Police,* the taller man dropped the bat and ran.
    II. I asked the girl for a description of the two men.
    III. I called for an ambulance.
    IV. A young girl approached me and stated that a man with a baseball bat was beating another man in front of 1700 Grande Street.
    V. Upon approaching the location, I observed the taller man hitting the other man with the bat.

The MOST logical order for the above sentences to appear in the report is

A. IV, V, I, II, III
B. V, IV, II, III, I
C. V, I, III, IV, II
D. IV, II, V, I, III

7. Police Officer Moore is writing a memobook entry concerning a summons he issued. The entry will contain the following five sentences:
   I. As I was walking down the platform, I heard music coming from a radio that a man was holding on his shoulder.
   II. I asked the man for some identification.
   III. I was walking in the subway when a passenger complained about a man playing a radio loudly at the opposite end of the station.
   IV. I then gave the man a summons for playing the radio. V. As soon as the man saw me approaching, he turned the radio off.
   The MOST logical order for the above sentences to appear in the memobook entry is

   A. III, V, II, I, IV
   B. I, II, V, IV, III
   C. III, I, V, II, IV
   D. I, V, II, IV, III

8. Police Officer Kashawahara is completing an Incident Report regarding fleeing suspects he had pursued earlier. The report will include the following five sentences:
   I. I saw two males attempting to break into a store through the front window.
   II. On Myrtle Avenue, they ran into an alley between two abandoned buildings.
   III. I yelled to them, *Hey, what are you guys doing by that window?*
   IV. At that time, I lost sight of the suspects and I returned to the station house.
   V. They started to run south on Wycoff Avenue heading towards Myrtle Avenue.
   The MOST logical order for the above sentences to appear in the report is

   A. I, V, II, IV, III
   B. III, V, II, IV, I
   C. I, III, V, II, IV
   D. III, I, V, II, IV

9. Police Officer Bloom is completing an entry in his memo-book regarding a confession made by a perpetrator. The entry will include the following five sentences:
   I. I went towards the dresser and took $400 in cash and a jewelry box with rings, watches, and other items in it.
   II. There in the bedroom, lying on the bed, a woman was sleeping.
   III. It was about 1:00 A.M. when I entered the apartment through an opened rear window.
   IV. I spun around, punched her in the face with my free hand, and then jumped out the window into the street.
   V. I walked back to the window carrying the money and the jewelry box and was about to go out when all of a sudden I heard the woman scream.
   The MOST logical order for the above sentences to appear in the memobook entry is

   A. I, III, II, V, IV
   B. I, V, IV, III, II
   C. III, II, I, V, IV
   D. III, V, IV, I, II

10. Police Officer Webster is preparing an Arrest Report which will include the following five sentences:
    I. I noticed that the robber had a knife placed at the victim's neck.
    II. I told the robber to drop the knife.
    III. While on patrol, I observed a robbery which was in progress.
    IV. I grabbed the robber, placed him in handcuffs, and took him to the precinct.
    V. The robber dropped the knife and tried to flee.
    The MOST logical order for the above sentences to appear in the report is

    A. I, II, V, IV, III
    B. III, I, II, V, IV
    C. III, II, IV, I, V
    D. I, III, IV, V, II

11. Police Officer Lee is preparing a report regarding someone who apparently attempted to commit suicide with a gun. The report will include the following five sentences:
   I. At the location, the woman pointed to the open door of Apartment 7L.
   II. I called for an ambulance to respond.
   III. The male had a gun in his hand and a large head wound.
   IV. A call was received from the radio dispatcher regarding a woman who heard a gunshot at 936 45th Avenue.
   V. Upon entering Apartment 7L, I saw the body of a male on the kitchen floor.

   The MOST logical order for the above sentences to appear in the report is

   A. IV, I, V, III, II
   B. I, III, V, IV, II
   C. I, V, III, II, IV
   D. IV, V, III, II, I

12. Police Officer Modrak is completing a memobook entry which will include the following five sentences:
   I. The victim, a male in his thirties, told me that the robbery occurred a few minutes ago.
   II. My partner and I jumped out of the patrol car and arrested the suspect.
   III. We responded to an armed robbery in progress at Billings Avenue and 59th Street.
   IV. On Chester Avenue and 68th Street, the victim spotted and identified the suspect.
   V. I told the victim to get into the patrol car and that we would drive him around the area.

   The MOST logical order for the above sentences to appear in the memobook is

   A. III, I, V, IV, II
   B. I, III, V, II, IV
   C. I, IV, III, V, II
   D. III, V, I, II, IV

13. Police Officer Rodriguez is preparing a report concerning an incident in which she used her revolver. Her report will include the following five sentences:
   I. Upon seeing my revolver, the robber dropped his gun to the ground.
   II. At about 10:55 P.M., I was informed by a passerby that several people were being robbed at gunpoint on 174th Street and Walton Avenue.
   III. I was assigned to patrol on 174th Street and Ghent Avenue during the evening shift.
   IV. I saw a man holding a gun on three people, took out my revolver, and shouted, *Police, don't move!*
   V. After calling for assistance, I went to 174th Street and Walton Avenue and took cover behind a car.

   The MOST logical order for the above sentences to appear in the report is

   A. II, III, IV, V, I
   B. IV, V, I, III, II
   C. III, II, V, IV, I
   D. II, IV, I, V, III

14. Police Officer Davis is completing an Activity Log entry which will include the following five sentences:
   I. A radio car was dispatched and the male was taken to Greenville Hospital.
   II. Several people saw him and called the police.
   III. A naked man was running down the street waving his arms above his head and screaming, *Insects are all over me!*
   IV. I arrived on the scene and requested an ambulance.
   V. The dispatcher informed me that no ambulances were available.

The MOST logical order for the above sentences to appear in the Activity Log is

A. III, IV, V, I, II
B. II, III, V, I, IV
C. III, II, IV, V, I
D. II, IV, III, V, I

15. Police Officer Peake is completing an entry in his Activity Log. The entry contains the following five sentences:
   I. He went to his parked car only to find he was blocked in.
   II. The owner of the vehicle refused to move the van until he had finished his lunch.
   III. Approximately 30 minutes later, I arrived on the scene and ordered the owner of the van to remove the vehicle.
   IV. Mr. O'Neil had an appointment and was in a hurry to keep it.
   V. Mr. O'Neil entered a nearby delicatessen and asked if anyone in there drove a dark blue van, license plate number BUS 265.

The MOST logical order for the above sentences to appear in the Activity Log is

A. II, III, I, IV, V
B. IV, I, V, II, III
C. V, IV, I, III, II
D. II, I, III, IV, V

16. Police Officer Harrison is preparing a report regarding a 10-year-old who was sexually abused at school. The report will include the following five sentences:
   I. The child described the perpetrator as a white male with a mustache, six feet tall, wearing a green uniform.
   II. On September 10, I responded to General Hospital to interview a child who was sexually abused.
   III. He later confessed at the station house.
   IV. After I interviewed the child, I responded to the school and found a janitor who fit the description.
   V. I interviewed the janitor and took him to the station house for further investigation.

The MOST logical order for the above sentences to appear in the report is

A. II, IV, I, V, III
B. I, IV, V, II, III
C. II, I, IV, V, III
D. V, III, II, I, IV

17. Police Officer Madden is completing a report of a theft. The report will include the following five sentences:
    I. I followed behind the suspect for two blocks.
    II. I saw a man pass by the radio car carrying a shopping bag.
    III. I looked back in the direction he had just come from and noticed that the top of a parking meter was missing.
    IV. As he saw me, he started to walk faster, and I noticed a red piece of metal with the word *violation* drop out of the shopping bag.
    V. When I saw a parking meter in the shopping bag, I apprehended the suspect and placed him under arrest.
    The MOST logical order for the above sentences to appear in the report is

    A. I, IV, II, III, V
    B. II, I, IV, V, III
    C. II, IV, III, I, V
    D. III, II, IV, I, V

17._____

18. Police Officer McCaslin is preparing a report of disorderly conduct which will include the following five sentences:
    I. Police Officer Kenny and I were on patrol in a radio car when we received a dispatch to go to the Hard Rock Disco on Third Avenue.
    II. We arrived at the scene and found three men arguing loudly and obviously intoxicated.
    III. The dispatcher had received a call from a bartender regarding a dispute.
    IV. Two of the men left the disco shortly before we did.
    V. We calmed the men down after managing to separate them.
    The MOST logical order for the above sentences to appear in the report is

    A. I, II, V, III, IV
    B. III, I, IV, II, V
    C. II, I, III, IV, V
    D. I, III, II, V, IV

18._____

19. Police Officer Langhorne is completing a report of a murder. The report will contain the following five statements made by a witness:
    I. The noise created by the roar of a motorcycle caused me to look out of my window.
    II. I ran out of the house and realized the man was dead, which is when I called the police.
    III. I saw a man driving at high speed down the dead-end street on a motorcycle, closely followed by a green BMW.
    IV. The motorcyclist then parked the bike and approached the car, which was occupied by two males.
    V. Two shots were fired and the cyclist fell to the ground; then the car made a u-turn and sped down the street.
    The MOST logical order for the above sentences to appear in the report is

    A. I, II, IV, III, V
    B. V, II, I, IV, III
    C. I, III, IV, V, II
    D. III, IV, I, II, V

19._____

20. Police Officer Murphy is preparing a report of a person who was assaulted. The report will include the following five sentences:
    I. I responded to the scene, but Mr. Jones had already fled.
    II. She was bleeding profusely from a cut above her right eye.
    III. Mr. and Mrs. Jones apparently were fighting in the street when Mr. Jones punched his wife in the face.
    IV. I then applied pressure to the cut to control the bleeding.
    V. I called the dispatcher on the radio to send an ambulance to respond to the scene.

    The MOST logical order for the above sentences to appear in the report is

    A. III, II, IV, I, V
    B. III, I, II, IV, V
    C. I, V, II, III, IV
    D. II, V, IV, III, I

20.____

KEY (CORRECT ANSWERS)

1. C
2. B
3. A
4. A
5. B

6. D
7. C
8. C
9. C
10. B

11. A
12. A
13. C
14. C
15. B

16. C
17. C
18. D
19. C
20. B

PHILOSOPHY, PRINCIPLES, PRACTICES, AND TECHNICS
OF
SUPERVISION, ADMINISTRATION, MANAGEMENT, AND ORGANIZATION

CONTENTS

	Page
I. MEANING OF SUPERVISION	1
II. THE OLD AND THE NEW SUPERVISION	1
III. THE EIGHT (8) BASIC PRINCIPLES OF THE NEW SUPERVISION	1
1. Principle of Responsibility	1
2. Principle of Authority	1
3. Principle of Self-Growth	1
4. Principle of Individual Worth	2
5. Principle of Creative Leadership	2
6. Principle of Success and Failure	2
7. Principle of Science	2
8. Principle of Cooperation	2
IV. WHAT IS ADMINISTRATION?	3
1. Practices Commonly Classed as "Supervisory"	3
2. Practices Commonly Classed as "Administrative"	3
3. Practices Classified as Both "Supervisory" and "Administrative"	3
V. RESPONSIBILITIES OF THE SUPERVISOR	3
VI. COMPETENCIES OF THE SUPERVISOR	4
VII. THE PROFESSIONAL SUPERVISOR-EMPLOYEE RELATIONSHIP	4
VIII. MINI-TEXT IN SUPERVISION, ADMINISTRATION, MANAGEMENT, AND ORGANIZATION	5
A. Brief Highlights	
1. Levels of Management	5
2. What the Supervisor Must Learn	5
3. A Definition of Supervision	6
4. Elements of the Team Concept	6
5. Principles of Organization	6
6. The Four Important Parts of Every Job	6
7. Principles of Delegation	6
8. Principles of Effective Communications	6
9. Principles of Work Improvement	6
10. Areas of Job Improvement	7
11. Seven Key Points in Making Improvements	7
12. Corrective Techniques of Job Improvement	7
13. A Planning Checklist	7
14. Five Characteristics of Good Directions	7
15. Types of Directions	8
16. Controls	8
17. Orienting the New Employee	8
18. Checklist for Orienting New Employees	8
19. Principles of Learning	8
20. Causes of Poor Performance	8
21. Four Major Steps in On-The-Job Instructions	8

CONTENTS (cont'd)

	Page
22. Employees Want Five Things	9
23. Some Don'ts in Regard to Praise	9
24. How to Gain Your Workers' Confidence	9
25. Sources of Employee Problems	9
26. The Supervisor's Key to Discipline	9
27. Five Important Processes of Management	10
28. When the Supervisor Fails to Plan	10
29. Fourteen General Principles of Management	10
30. Change	10
B. Brief Topical Summaries	11
I. Who/What is the Supervisor?	11
II. The Sociology of Work	11
III. Principles and Practices of Supervision	11
IV. Dynamic Leadership	12
V. Processes for Solving Problems	12
VI. Training for Results	13
VII. Health, Safety, and Accident Prevention	13
VIII. Equal Employment Opportunity	13
IX. Improving Communications	14
X. Self-Development	14
XI. Teaching and Training	14
A. The Teaching Process	14
1. Preparation	15
2. Presentation	15
3. Summary	15
4. Application	15
5. Evaluation	15
B. Teaching Methods	15
1. Lecture	16
2. Discussion	16
3. Demonstration	16
4. Performance	16
5. Which Method to Use	16

PHILOSOPHY, PRINCIPLES, PRACTICES, AND TECHNICS
OF
SUPERVISION, ADMINISTRATION, MANAGEMENT, AND ORGANIZATION

I. MEANING OF SUPERVISION

The extension of the democratic philosophy has been accompanied by an extension in the scope of supervision. Modern leaders and supervisors no longer think of supervision in the narrow sense of being confined chiefly to visiting employees, supplying materials, or rating the staff. They regard supervision as being intimately related to all the concerned agencies of society, they speak of the supervisor's function in terms of "growth", rather than the "improvement," of employees

This modern concept of supervision may be defined as follows:

Supervision is leadership and the development of leadership within groups which are cooperatively engaged in inspection, research, training, guidance and evaluation.

II. THE OLD AND THE NEW SUPERVISION

TRADITIONAL	MODERN
1. Inspection	1. Study and analysis
2. Focused on the employee	2. Focused on aims, materials, methods, supervisors, employees, environment
3. Visitation	3. Demonstrations, intervisitation, workshops, directed reading, bulletins, etc.
4. Random and haphazard	4. Definitely organized and planned (scientific)
5. Imposed and authoritarian	5. Cooperative and democratic
6. One person usually	6. Many persons involved (creative)

III. THE EIGHT (8) BASIC PRINCIPLES OF THE NEW SUPERVISION

1. *PRINCIPLE OF RESPONSIBILITY*

   Authority to act and responsibility for acting must be joined.
   a. If you give responsibility, give authority.
   b. Define employee duties clearly.
   c. Protect employees from criticism by others.
   d. Recognize the rights as well as obligations of employees.
   e. Achieve the aims of a democratic society insofar as it is possible within the area of your work.
   f. Establish a situation favorable to training and learning.
   g. Accept ultimate responsibility for everything done in your section, unit, office, division, department.
   h. Good administration and good supervision are inseparable.

2. *PRINCIPLE OF AUTHORITY*

   The success of the supervisor is measured by the extent to which the power of authority is not used.
   a. Exercise simplicity and informality in supervision.
   b. Use the simplest machinery of supervision.
   c. If it is good for the organization as a whole, it is probably justified.
   d. Seldom be arbitrary or authoritative.
   e. Do not base your work on the power of position or of personality.
   f. Permit and encourage the free expression of opinions.

3. *PRINCIPLE OF SELF-GROWTH*

   The success of the supervisor is measured by the extent to which, and the speed with which, he is no longer needed.
   a. Base criticism on principles, not on specifics.
   b. Point out higher activities to employees.

      c. Train for self-thinking by employees, to meet new situations.
      d. Stimulate initiative, self-reliance and individual responsibility.
      e. Concentrate on stimulating the growth of employees rather than on removing defects.
4. *PRINCIPLE OF INDIVIDUAL WORTH*
   Respect for the individual is a paramount consideration in supervision.
      a. Be human and sympathetic in dealing with employees.
      b. Don't nag about things to be done.
      c. Recognize the individual differences among employees and seek opportunities to permit best expression of each personality.
5. *PRINCIPLE OF CREATIVE LEADERSHIP*
   The best supervision is that which is not apparent to the employee.
      a. Stimulate, don't drive employees to creative action.
      b. Emphasize doing good things.
      c. Encourage employees to do what they do best.
      d. Do not be too greatly concerned with details of subject or method.
      e. Do not be concerned exclusively with immediate problems and activities.
      f. Reveal higher activities and make them both desired and maximally possible.
      g. Determine procedures in the light of each situation but see that these are derived from a sound basic philosophy.
      h. Aid, inspire and lead so as to liberate the creative spirit latent in all good employees.
6. *PRINCIPLE OF SUCCESS AND FAILURE*
   There are no unsuccessful employees, only unsuccessful supervisors who have failed to give proper leadership.
      a. Adapt suggestions to the capacities, attitudes, and prejudices of employees.
      b. Be gradual, be progressive, be persistent.
      c. Help the employee find the general principle; have the employee apply his own problem to the general principle.
      d. Give adequate appreciation for good work and honest effort.
      e. Anticipate employee difficulties and help to prevent them.
      f. Encourage employees to do the desirable things they will do anyway.
      g. Judge your supervision by the results it secures.
7. *PRINCIPLE OF SCIENCE*
   Successful supervision is scientific, objective, and experimental. It is based on facts, not on prejudices.
      a. Be cumulative in results.
      b. Never divorce your suggestions from the goals of training.
      c. Don't be impatient of results.
      d. Keep all matters on a professional, not a personal level.
      e. Do not be concerned exclusively with immediate problems and activities.
      f. Use objective means of determining achievement and rating where possible.
8. *PRINCIPLE OF COOPERATION*
   Supervision is a cooperative enterprise between supervisor and employee.
      a. Begin with conditions as they are.
      b. Ask opinions of all involved when formulating policies.

      c. Organization is as good as its weakest link.
      d. Let employees help to determine policies and department programs.
      e. Be approachable and accessible - physically and mentally.
      f. Develop pleasant social relationships.

IV. WHAT IS ADMINISTRATION?

Administration is concerned with providing the environment, the material facilities, and the operational procedures that will promote the maximum growth and development of supervisors and employees. (Organization is an aspect, and a concomitant, of administration.)

There is no sharp line of demarcation between supervision and administration; these functions are intimately interrelated and, often, overlapping. They are complementary activities.

1. *PRACTICES COMMONLY CLASSED AS "SUPERVISORY"*
   a. Conducting employees conferences
   b. Visiting sections, units, offices, divisions, departments
   c. Arranging for demonstrations
   d. Examining plans
   e. Suggesting professional reading
   f. Interpreting bulletins
   g. Recommending in-service training courses
   h. Encouraging experimentation
   i. Appraising employee morale
   j. Providing for intervisitation

2. *PRACTICES COMMONLY CLASSIFIED AS "ADMINISTRATIVE"*
   a. Management of the office
   b. Arrangement of schedules for extra duties
   c. Assignment of rooms or areas
   d. Distribution of supplies
   e. Keeping records and reports
   f. Care of audio-visual materials
   g. Keeping inventory records
   h. Checking record cards and books
   i. Programming special activities
   j. Checking on the attendance and punctuality of employees

3. *PRACTICES COMMONLY CLASSIFIED AS BOTH "SUPERVISORY" AND "ADMINISTRATIVE"*
   a. Program construction
   b. Testing or evaluating outcomes
   c. Personnel accounting
   d. Ordering instructional materials

V. RESPONSIBILITIES OF THE SUPERVISOR

A person employed in a supervisory capacity must constantly be able to improve his own efficiency and ability. He represents the employer to the employees and only continuous self-examination can make him a capable supervisor.

Leadership and training are the supervisor's responsibility. An efficient working unit is one in which the employees work with the supervisor. It is his job to bring out the best in his employees. He must always be relaxed, courteous and calm in his association with his employees. Their feelings are important, and a harsh attitude does not develop the most efficient employees.

VI. COMPETENCIES OF THE SUPERVISOR
1. Complete knowledge of the duties and responsibilities of his position.
2. To be able to organize a job, plan ahead and carry through.
3. To have self-confidence and initiative.
4. To be able to handle the unexpected situation and make quick decisions.
5. To be able to properly train subordinates in the positions they are best suited for.
6. To be able to keep good human relations among his subordinates.
7. To be able to keep good human relations between his subordinates and himself and to earn their respect and trust.

VII. THE PROFESSIONAL SUPERVISOR-EMPLOYEE RELATIONSHIP

There are two kinds of efficiency: one kind is only apparent and is produced in organizations through the exercise of mere discipline; this is but a simulation of the second, or true, efficiency which springs from spontaneous cooperation. If you are a manager, no matter how great or small your responsibility, it is your job, in the final analysis, to create and develop this involuntary cooperation among the people whom you supervise. For, no matter how powerful a combination of money, machines, and materials a company may have, this is a dead and sterile thing without a team of willing, thinking and articulate people to guide it.

The following 21 points are presented as indicative of the exemplary basic relationship that should exist between supervisor and employee:

1. Each person wants to be liked and respected by his fellow employee and wants to be treated with consideration and respect by his superior.
2. The most competent employee will make an error. However, in a unit where good relations exist between the supervisor and his employees, tenseness and fear do not exist. Thus, errors are not hidden or covered up and the efficiency of a unit is not impaired.
3. Subordinates resent rules, regulations, or orders that are unreasonable or unexplained.
4. Subordinates are quick to resent unfairness, harshness, injustices and favoritism.
5. An employee will accept responsibility if he knows that he will be complimented for a job well done, and not too harshly chastized for failure; that his supervisor will check the cause of the failure, and, if it was the supervisor's fault, he will assume the blame therefor. If it was the employee's fault, his supervisor will explain the correct method or means of handling the responsibility.
6. An employee wants to receive credit for a suggestion he has made, that is used. If a suggestion cannot be used, the employee is entitled to an explanation. The supervisor should not say "no" and close the subject.
7. Fear and worry slow up a worker's ability. Poor working environment can impair his physical and mental health. A good supervisor avoids forceful methods, threats and arguments to get a job done.
8. A forceful supervisor is able to train his employees individually and as a team, and is able to motivate them in the proper channels.

9. A mature supervisor is able to properly evaluate his subordinates and to keep them happy and satisfied.
10. A sensitive supervisor will never patronize his subordinates.
11. A worthy supervisor will respect his employees' confidences.
12. Definite and clear-cut responsibilities should be assigned to each executive.
13. Responsibility should always be coupled with corresponding authority.
14. No change should be made in the scope or responsibilities of a position without a definite understanding to that effect on the part of all persons concerned.
15. No executive or employee, occupying a single position in the organization, should be subject to definite orders from more than one source.
16. Orders should never be given to subordinates over the head of a responsible executive. Rather than do this, the officer in question should be supplanted.
17. Criticisms of subordinates should, whever possible, be made privately, and in no case should a subordinate be criticized in the presence of executives or employees of equal or lower rank.
18. No dispute or difference between executives or employees as to authority or responsibilities should be considered too trivial for prompt and careful adjudication.
19. Promotions, wage changes, and disciplinary action should always be approved by the executive immediately superior to the one directly responsible.
20. No executive or employee should ever be required, or expected, to be at the same time an assistant to, and critic of, another.
21. Any executive whose work is subject to regular inspection should, whever practicable, be given the assistance and facilities necessary to enable him to maintain an independent check of the quality of his work.

VIII. MINI-TEXT IN SUPERVISION, ADMINISTRATION, MANAGEMENT, AND ORGANIZATION
A. BRIEF HIGHLIGHTS
Listed concisely and sequentially are major headings and important data in the field for quick recall and review.

1. *LEVELS OF MANAGEMENT*

    Any organization of some size has several levels of management. In terms of a ladder the levels are:

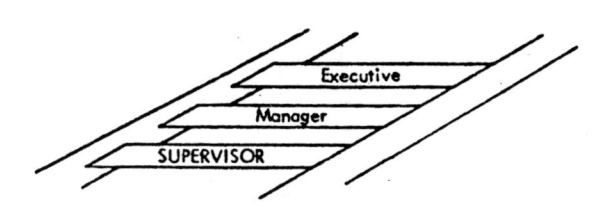

    Executive
    Manager
    SUPERVISOR

    The first level is very important because it is the beginning point of management leadership.

2. *WHAT THE SUPERVISOR MUST LEARN*

    A supervisor must learn to:
    (1) Deal with people and their differences
    (2) Get the job done through people
    (3) Recognize the problems when they exist
    (4) Overcome obstacles to good performance
    (5) Evaluate the performance of people
    (6) Check his own performance in terms of accomplishment

3. *A DEFINITION OF SUPERVISOR*
   The term supervisor means any individual having authority, in the interests of the employer, to hire,transfer,suspend,lay-off,recall, promote,discharge,assign,reward,or discipline other employees... or responsibility to direct them,or to adjust their grievances,or effectively to recommend such action,if, in connection with the foregoing, exercise of such authority is not of a merely routine or clerical nature but requires the use of independent judgment.
4. *ELEMENTS OF THE TEAM CONCEPT*
   What is involved in teamwork? The component parts are:
   (1) Members   (3) Goals   (5) Cooperation
   (2) A leader   (4) Plans   (6) Spirit
5. *PRINCIPLES OF ORGANIZATION*
   (1) A team member must know what his job is
   (2) Be sure that the nature and scope of a job are understood
   (3) Authority and responsibility should be carefully spelled out
   (4) A supervisor should be permitted to make the maximum number of decisions affecting his employees
   (5) Employees should report to only one supervisor
   (6) A supervisor should direct only as many employees as he can handle effectively
   (7) An organization plan should be flexible
   (8) Inspection and performance of work should be separate
   (9) Organizational problems should receive immediate attention
   (10) Assign work in line with ability and experience
6. *THE FOUR IMPORTANT PARTS OF EVERY JOB*
   (1) Inherent in every job is the *accountability* for results
   (2) A second set of factors in every job are *responsibilities*
   (3) Along with duties and responsibilities one must have the *authority* to act within certain limits without obtaining permission to proceed
   (4) No job exists in a vacuum. The supervisor is surrounded by key *relationships*
7. *PRINCIPLES OF DELEGATION*
   Where work is delegated for the first time,the supervisor should think in terms of these questions:
   (1) Who is best qualified to do this?
   (2) Can an employee improve his abilities by doing this?
   (3) How long should an employee spend on this?
   (4) Are there any special problems for which he will need guidance?
   (5) How broad a delegation can I make?
8. *PRINCIPLES OF EFFECTIVE COMMUNICATIONS*
   (1) Determine the media
   (2) To whom directed?
   (3) Identification and source authority
   (4) Is communication understood?
9. *PRINCIPLES OF WORK IMPROVEMENT*
   (1) Most people usually do only the work which is assigned to them
   (2) Workers are likely to fit assigned work into the time available to perform it
   (3) A good workload usually stimulates output
   (4) People usually do their best work when they know that results will be reviewed or inspected

   (5) Employees usually feel that someone else is responsible for conditions of work, workplace layout, job methods, type of tools and equipment, and other such factors
   (6) Employees are usually defensive about their job security
   (7) Employees have natural resistance to change
   (8) Employees can support or destroy a supervisor
   (9) A supervisor usually earns the respect of his people through his personal example of diligence and efficiency

10. *AREAS OF JOB IMPROVEMENT*

  The *areas* of job improvement are quite numerous, but the most common ones which a supervisor can identify and utilize are:
   (1) Departmental layout (5) Work methods
   (2) Flow of work   (6) Materials handling
   (3) Workplace layout   (7) Utilization
   (4) Utilization of manpower (8) Motion economy

11. *SEVEN KEY POINTS IN MAKING IMPROVEMENTS*
   (1) Select the job to be improved
   (2) Study how it is being done now
   (3) Question the present method
   (4) Determine actions to be taken
   (5) Chart proposed method
   (6) Get approval and apply
   (7) Solicit worker participation

12. *CORRECTIVE TECHNIQUES OF JOB IMPROVEMENT*

Specific Problems	*General Problems*	*Corrective Technique*
(1) Size of workload	(1) Departmental layout	(1) Study with scale model
(2) Inability to meet schedules	(2) Flow of work	(2) Flow chart study
(3) Strain and fatigue	(3) Workplan layout	(3) Motion analysis
(4) Improper use of men and skills	(4) Utilization of manpower	(4) Comparison of units produced to standard allowances
(5) Waste, poor quality, unsafe conditions	(5) Work methods	(5) Methods analysis
(6) Bottleneck conditions that hinder output	(6) Materials handling	(6) Flow chart and equipment study
(7) Poor utilization of equipment and machines	(7) Utilization of equipment	(7) Down time vs. running time
(8) Efficiency and productivity of labor	(8) Motion economy	(8) Motion analysis

13. *A PLANNING CHECKLIST*
   (1) Objectives   (8) Equipment
   (2) Controls   (9) Supplies and materials
   (3) Delegations   (10) Utilization of time
   (4) Communications   (11) Safety
   (5) Resources   (12) Money
   (6) Methods and procedures (13) Work
   (7) Manpower   (14) Timing of improvements

14. *FIVE CHARACTERISTICS OF GOOD DIRECTIONS*
  In order to get results, directions must be:
   (1) Possible of accomplishment (4) Planned and complete
   (2) Agreeable with worker interests (5) Unmistakably clear
   (3) Related to mission

15. *TYPES OF DIRECTIONS*
    (1) Demands or direct orders (3) Suggestion or implication
    (2) Requests   (4) Volunteering
16. *CONTROLS*
    A typical listing of the overall areas in which the supervisor should establish controls might be:
    (1) Manpower   (4) Quantity of work   (7) Money
    (2) Materials   (5) Time   (8) Methods
    (3) Quality of work (6) Space
17. *ORIENTING THE NEW EMPLOYEE*
    (1) Prepare for him   (3) Orientation for the job
    (2) Welcome the new employee (4) Follow-up
18. *CHECKLIST FOR ORIENTING NEW EMPLOYEES*

                                                                                     Yes No

    (1) Do your appreciate the feelings of new employees when they first report for work?
    (2) Are you aware of the fact that the new employee must make a big adjustment to his job?
    (3) Have you given him good reasons for liking the job and the organization?
    (4) Have you prepared for his first day on the job?
    (5) Did you welcome him cordially and make him feel needed?
    (6) Did you establish rapport with him so that he feels free to talk and discuss matters with you?
    (7) Did you explain his job to him and his relationship to you?
    (8) Does he know that his work will be evaluated periodically on a basis that is fair and objective?
    (9) Did you introduce him to his fellow workers in such a way that they are likely to accept him?
    (10) Does he know what employee benefits he will receive?
    (11) Does he understand the importance of being on the job and what to do if he must leave his duty station?
    (12) Has he been impressed with the importance of accident prevention and safe practice?
    (13) Does he generally know his way around the department?
    (14) Is he under the guidance of a sponsor who will teach the right ways of doing things?
    (15) Do you plan to follow-up so that he will continue to adjust successfully to his job?
19. *PRINCIPLES OF LEARNING*
    (1) Motivation   (2) Demonstration or explanation
    (3) Practice
20. *CAUSES OF POOR PERFORMANCE*
    (1) Improper training for job   (6) Lack of standards of
    (2) Wrong tools   performance
    (3) Inadequate directions   (7) Wrong work habits
    (4) Lack of supervisory follow-up   (8) Low morale
    (5) Poor communications   (9) Other
21. *FOUR MAJOR STEPS IN ON-THE-JOB INSTRUCTION*
    (1) Prepare the worker   (3) Tryout performance
    (2) Present the operation (4) Follow-up

22. *EMPLOYEES WANT FIVE THINGS*
    (1) Security   (2) Opportunity (3) Recognition
    (4) Inclusion (5) Expression
23. *SOME DON'TS IN REGARD TO PRAISE*
    (1) Don't praise a person for something he hasn't done
    (2) Don't praise a person unless you can be sincere
    (3) Don't be sparing in praise just because your superior withholds it from you
    (4) Don't let too much time elapse between good performance and recognition of it
24. *HOW TO GAIN YOUR WORKERS' CONFIDENCE*
    Methods of developing confidence include such things as:
    (1) Knowing the interests, habits, hobbies of employees
    (2) Admitting your own inadequacies
    (3) Sharing and telling of confidence in others
    (4) Supporting people when they are in trouble
    (5) Delegating matters that can be well handled
    (6) Being frank and straightforward about problems and working conditions
    (7) Encouraging others to bring their problems to you
    (8) Taking action on problems which impede worker progress
25. *SOURCES OF EMPLOYEE PROBLEMS*
    On-the-job causes might be such things as:
    (1) A feeling that favoritism is exercised in assignments
    (2) Assignment of overtime
    (3) An undue amount of supervision
    (4) Changing methods or systems
    (5) Stealing of ideas or trade secrets
    (6) Lack of interest in job
    (7) Threat of reduction in force
    (8) Ignorance or lack of communications
    (9) Poor equipment
    (10) Lack of knowing how supervisor feels toward employee
    (11) Shift assignments
    Off-the-job problems might have to do with:
    (1) Health (2) Finances (3) Housing (4) Family
26. *THE SUPERVISOR'S KEY TO DISCIPLINE*
    There are several key points about discipline which the supervisor should keep in mind:
    (1) Job discipline is one of the disciplines of life and is directed by the supervisor.
    (2) It is more important to correct an employee fault than to fix blame for it.
    (3) Employee performance is affected by problems both on the job and off.
    (4) Sudden or abrupt changes in behavior can be indications of important employee problems.
    (5) Problems should be dealt with as soon as possible after they are identified.
    (6) The attitude of the supervisor may have more to do with solving problems than the techniques of problem solving.
    (7) Correction of employee behavior should be resorted to only after the supervisor is sure that training or counseling will not be helpful
    (8) Be sure to document your disciplinary actions.

(9) Make sure that you are disciplining on the basis of facts rather than personal feelings.
(10) Take each disciplinary step in order, being careful not to make snap judgments, or decisions based on impatience.

27. *FIVE IMPORTANT PROCESSES OF MANAGEMENT*
    (1) Planning   (2) Organizing   (3) Scheduling
    (4) Controlling   (5) Motivating

28. *WHEN THE SUPERVISOR FAILS TO PLAN*
    (1) Supervisor creates impression of not knowing his job
    (2) May lead to excessive overtime
    (3) Job runs itself-- supervisor lacks control
    (4) Deadlines and appointments missed
    (5) Parts of the work go undone
    (6) Work interrupted by emergencies
    (7) Sets a bad example
    (8) Uneven workload creates peaks and valleys
    (9) Too much time on minor details at expense of more important tasks

29. *FOURTEEN GENERAL PRINCIPLES OF MANAGEMENT*
    (1) Division of work   (8) Centralization
    (2) Authority and responsibility (9) Scalar chain
    (3) Discipline   (10) Order
    (4) Unity of command   (11) Equity
    (5) Unity of direction   (12) Stability of tenure of
    (6) Subordination of individual   personnel
        interest to general interest (13) Initiative
    (7) Remuneration of personnel   (14) Esprit de corps

30. *CHANGE*
    Bringing about change is perhaps attempted more often, and yet less well understood, than anything else the supervisor does. How do people generally react to change? (People tend to resist change that is imposed upon them by other individuals or circumstances.)
    Change is characteristic of every situation. It is a part of every real endeavor where the efforts of people are concerned.
    A. Why do people resist change?
       People may resist change because of:
       (1) Fear of the unknown
       (2) Implied criticism
       (3) Unpleasant experiences in the past
       (4) Fear of loss of status
       (5) Threat to the ego
       (6) Fear of loss of economic stability
    B. How can we best overcome the resistance to change?
       In initiating change, take these steps:
       (1) Get ready to sell
       (2) identify sources of help
       (3) Anticipate objections
       (4) Sell benefits
       (5) Listen in depth
       (6) Follow up

B. BRIEF TOPICAL SUMMARIES

I. WHO/WHAT IS THE SUPERVISOR?
1. The supervisor is often called the "highest level employee and the lowest level manager."
2. A supervisor is a member of both management and the work group. He acts as a bridge between the two.
3. Most problems in supervision are in the area of human relations, or people problems.
4. Employees expect: Respect, opportunity to learn and to advance, and a sense of belonging, and so forth.
5. Supervisors are responsible for directing people and organizing work. Planning is of paramount importance.
6. A position description is a set of duties and responsibilities inherent to a given position.
7. It is important to keep the position description up-to-date and to provide each employee with his own copy.

II. THE SOCIOLOGY OF WORK
1. People are alike in many ways; however each individual is unique.
2. The supervisor is challenged in getting to know employee differences. Acquiring skills in evaluating individuals is an asset.
3. Maintaining meaningful working relationships in the organization is of great importance.
4. The supervisor has an obligation to help individuals to develop to their fullest potential.
5. Job rotation on a planned basis helps to build versatility and to maintain interest and enthusiasm in work groups.
6. Cross training (job rotation) provides backup skills.
7. The supervisor can help reduce tension by maintaining a sense of humor, providing guidance to employees, and by making reasonable and timely decisions. Employees respond favorably to working under reasonably predictable circumstances.
8. Change is characteristic of all managerial behavior. The supervisor must adjust to changes in procedures, new methods, technological changes, and to a number of new and sometimes challenging situations.
9. To overcome the natural tendency for people to resist change, the supervisor should become more skillful in initiating change.

III. PRINCIPLES AND PRACTICES OF SUPERVISION
1. Employees should be required to answer to only one superior.
2. A supervisor can effectively direct only a limited number of employees, depending upon the complexity, variety, and proximity of the jobs involved.
3. The organizational chart presents the organization in graphic form. It reflects lines of authority and responsibility as well as interrelationships of units within the organization.
4. Distribution of work can be improved through an analysis using the "Work Distribution Chart."
5. The "Work Distribution Chart" reflects the division of work within a unit in understandable form.
6. When related tasks are given to an employee, he has a better chance of increasing his skills through training.
7. The individual who is given the responsibility for tasks must also be given the appropriate authority to insure adequate results.
8. The supervisor should delegate repetitive, routine work. Preparation of recurring reports, maintaining leave and attendance records are some examples.

11

9. Good discipline is essential to good task performance. Discipline is reflected in the actions of employees on the job in the absence of supervision.
10. Disciplinary action may have to be taken when the positive aspects of discipline have failed. Reprimand, warning, and suspension are examples of disciplinary action.
11. If a situation calls for a reprimand, be sure it is deserved and remember it is to be done in private.

IV. DYNAMIC LEADERSHIP
1. A style is a personal method or manner of exerting influence.
2. Authoritarian leaders often see themselves as the source of power and authority.
3. The democratic leader often perceives the group as the source of authority and power.
4. Supervisors tend to do better when using the pattern of leadership that is most natural for them.
5. Social scientists suggest that the effective supervisor use the leadership style that best fits the problem or circumstances involved.
6. All four styles -- telling, selling, consulting, joining -- have their place. Using one does not preclude using the other at another time.
7. The theory X point of view assumes that the average person dislikes work, will avoid it whenever possible, and must be coerced to achieve organizational objectives.
8. The theory Y point of view assumes that the average person considers work to be as natural as play, and, when the individual is committed, he requires little supervision or direction to accomplish desired objectives.
9. The leader's basic assumptions concerning human behavior and human nature affect his actions, decisions, and other managerial practices.
10. Dissatisfaction among employees is often present, but difficult to isolate. The supervisor should seek to weaken dissatisfaction by keeping promises, being sincere and considerate, keeping employees informed, and so forth.
11. Constructive suggestions should be encouraged during the natural progress of the work.

V. PROCESSES FOR SOLVING PROBLEMS
1. People find their daily tasks more meaningful and satisfying when they can improve them.
2. The causes of problems, or the key factors, are often hidden in the background. Ability to solve problems often involves the ability to isolate them from their backgrounds. There is some substance to the cliché that some persons "can't see the forest for the trees."
3. New procedures are often developed from old ones. Problems should be broken down into manageable parts. New ideas can be adapted from old ones.
4. People think differently in problem-solving situations. Using a logical, patterned approach is often useful. One approach found to be useful includes these steps:
   (a) Define the problem   (d) Weigh and decide
   (b) Establish objectives (e) Take action
   (c) Get the facts   (f) Evaluate action

VI. TRAINING FOR RESULTS

1. Participants respond best when they feel training is important to them.
2. The supervisor has responsibility for the training and development of those who report to him.
3. When training is delegated to others, great care must be exercised to insure the trainer has knowledge, aptitude, and interest for his work as a trainer.
4. Training (learning) of some type goes on continually. The most successful supervisor makes certain the learning contributes in a productive manner to operational goals.
5. New employees are particularly susceptible to training. Older employees facing new job situations require specific training, as well as having need for development and growth opportunities.
6. Training needs require continuous monitoring.
7. The training officer of an agency is a professional with a responsibility to assist supervisors in solving training problems.
8. Many of the self-development steps important to the supervisor's own growth are equally important to the development of peers and subordinates. Knowledge of these is important when the supervisor consults with others on development and growth opportunities.

VII. HEALTH, SAFETY, AND ACCIDENT PREVENTION

1. Management-minded supervisors take appropriate measures to assist employees in maintaining health and in assuring safe practices in the work environment.
2. Effective safety training and practices help to avoid injury and accidents.
3. Safety should be a management goal. All infractions of safety which are observed should be corrected without exception.
4. Employees' safety attitude, training and instruction, provision of safe tools and equipment, supervision, and leadership are considered highly important factors which contribute to safety and which can be influenced directly by supervisors.
5. When accidents do occur they should be investigated promptly for very important reasons, including the fact that information which is gained can be used to prevent accidents in the future.

VIII. EQUAL EMPLOYMENT OPPORTUNITY

1. The supervisor should endeavor to treat all employees fairly, without regard to religion, race, sex, or national origin.
2. Groups tend to reflect the attitude of the leader. Prejudice can be detected even in very subtle form. Supervisors must strive to create a feeling of mutual respect and confidence in every employee.
3. Complete utilization of all human resources is a national goal. Equitable consideration should be accorded women in the work force, minority-group members, the physically and mentally handicapped, and the older employee. The important question is: "Who can do the job?"
4. Training opportunities, recognition for performance, overtime assignments, promotional opportunities, and all other personnel actions are to be handled on an equitable basis.

IX. IMPROVING COMMUNICATIONS
   1. Communications is achieving understanding between the sender and the receiver of a message. It also means sharing information -- the creation of understanding.
   2. Communication is basic to all human activity. Words are means of conveying meanings; however, real meanings are in people.
   3. There are very practical differences in the effectiveness of one-way, impersonal, and two-way communications. Words spoken face-to-face are better understood. Telephone conversations are effective, but lack the rapport of person-to-person exchanges. The whole person communicates.
   4. Cooperation and communication in an organization go hand-in-hand. When there is a mutual respect between people, spelling out rules and procedures for communicating is unnecessary.
   5. There are several barriers to effective communications. These include failure to listen with respect and understanding, lack of skill in feedback, and misinterpreting the meanings of words used by the speaker. It is also common practice to listen to what we want to hear, and tune out things we do not want to hear.
   6. Communication is management's chief problem. The supervisor should accept the challenge to communicate more effectively and to improve interagency and intra-agency communications.
   7. The supervisor may often plan for and conduct meetings. The planning phase is critical and may determine the success or the failure of a meeting.
   8. Speaking before groups usually requires extra effort. Stage fright may never disappear completely, but it can be controlled.

X. SELF-DEVELOPMENT
   1. Every employee is responsible for his own self-development.
   2. Toastmaster and toastmistress clubs offer opportunities to improve skills in oral communications.
   3. Planning for one's own self-development is of vital importance. Supervisors know their own strengths and limitations better than anyone else.
   4. Many opportunities are open to aid the supervisor in his developmental efforts, including job assignments; training opportunities, both governmental and non-governmental -- to include universities and professional conferences and seminars.
   5. Programmed instruction offers a means of studying at one's own rate.
   6. Where difficulties may arise from a supervisor's being away from his work for training, he may participate in televised home study or correspondence courses to meet his self-development needs.

XI. TEACHING AND TRAINING
   A. The Teaching Process
      Teaching is encouraging and guiding the learning activities of students toward established goals. In most cases this process consists in five steps: preparation, presentation, summarization, evaluation, and application.

1. Preparation
    Preparation is twofold in nature; that of the supervisor and the employee.
    Preparation by the supervisor is absolutely essential to success. He must know what, when, where, how, and whom he will teach. Some of the factors that should be considered are:
    (1) The objectives   (5) Employee interest
    (2) The materials needed (6) Training aids
    (3) The methods to be used (7) Evaluation
    (4) Employee participation (8) Summarization
    Employee preparation consists in preparing the employee to receive the material. Probably the most important single factor in the preparation of the employee is arousing and maintaining his interest. He must know the objectives of the training, why he is there, how the material can be used, and its importance to him.
2. Presentation
    In presentation, have a carefully designed plan and follow it. The plan should be accurate and complete, yet flexible enough to meet situations as they arise. The method of presentation will be determined by the particular situation and objectives.
3. Summary
    A summary should be made at the end of every training unit and program. In addition, there may be internal summaries depending on the nature of the material being taught. The important thing is that the trainee must always be able to understand how each part of the new material relates to the whole.
4. Application
    The supervisor must arrange work so the employee will be given a chance to apply new knowledge or skills while the material is still clear in his mind and interest is high. The trainee does not really know whether he has learned the material until he has been given a chance to apply it. If the material is not applied, it loses most of its value.
5. Evaluation
    The purpose of all training is to promote learning. To determine whether the training has been a success or failure, the supervisor must evaluate this learning.
    In the broadest sense evaluation includes all the devices, methods, skills, and techniques used by the supervisor to keep himself and the employees informed as to their progress toward the objectives they are pursuing. The extent to which the employee has mastered the knowledge, skills, and abilities, or changed his attitudes, as determined by the program objectives, is the extent to which instruction has succeeded or failed.
    Evaluation should not be confined to the end of the lesson, day, or program but should be used continuously. We shall note later the way this relates to the rest of the teaching process.

B. Teaching Methods
    A teaching method is a pattern of identifiable student and instructor activity used in presenting training material.
    All supervisors are faced with the problem of deciding which method should be used at a given time.

1. Lecture
   The lecture is direct oral presentation of material by the supervisor. The present trend is to place less emphasis on the trainer's activity and more on that of the trainee.
2. Discussion
   Teaching by discussion or conference involves using questions and other techniques to arouse interest and focus attention upon certain areas, and by doing so creating a learning situation. This can be one of the most valuable methods because it gives the employees an opportunity to express their ideas and pool their knowledge.
3. Demonstration
   The demonstration is used to teach how something works or how to do something. It can be used to show a principle or what the results of a series of actions will be. A well-staged demonstration is particularly effective because it shows proper methods of performance in a realistic manner.
4. Performance
   Performance is one of the most fundamental of all learning techniques or teaching methods. The trainee may be able to tell how a specific operation should be performed but he cannot be sure he knows how to perform the operation until he has done so.

As with all methods, there are certain advantages and disadvantages to each method.

5. Which Method to Use
   Moreover, there are other methods and techniques of teaching. It is difficult to use any method without other methods entering into it. In any learning situation a combination of methods is usually more effective than any one method alone.

Finally, evaluation must be integrated into the other aspects of the teaching-learning process.
It must be used in the motivation of the trainees; it must be used to assist in developing understanding during the training; and it must be related to employee application of the results of training.
This is distinctly the role of the supervisor.

DISASTER PREPAREDNESS

Table of Contents

```
IMMEDIATE RESPONSE..............................1
    Alert.......................................1
    Assessment..................................2
    Action......................................4

FISCAL..........................................6

PREPLANNING.....................................8
    Considerations in Developing Disaster
        Response Plan...........................8
    Coordination Efforts........................8
    Operational Procedure Development...........9
    Identification of Numbers of Elderly
        Affected................................9
    Communications.............................10
    Supplies...................................13
    Training...................................15
    Services...................................17
        Independent Appraiser..................20
        Advocacy...............................21
        Legal Assistance.......................23
        Transportation.........................24
        Homemaker/Chore........................26
        Handiman...............................27
        Outreach...............................28
        Meals..................................29
    Long-term Services.........................30
    Personnel..................................31
        Disaster Preparedness Coordinator......31
        Considerations in Planning.............31
        Developing Personnel Section...........32
        Disaster Cadre.........................32

DISASTER ASSISTANCE CENTER.....................33
    Overview...................................33
    AAA Role...................................35
    Resources Available from Selected
        Disaster Relief Agencies...............37
        Temporary Housing......................37
        Legal Assistance.......................38
        Emergency Food Stamp Program...........38
        American Red Cross.....................39
        Mennonite Disaster Service.............39
        Tax Information........................39
        Unemployment Assistance................40
        Home Repair Loans......................40
        Salvation Army.........................40
        Individual and Family Grants...........41
```

(Contents Cont'd)

APPENDICES
    Aspects of Disaster Response Particular
        to Specific Catagories of Disasters......42
    Sample Client Contact/Intake/follow-
        up Forms................................47
    Lists of Possible Losses.....................50

DISASTER PREPAREDNESS
DISASTER HITS (IMMEDIATE RESPONSE)

Alert

Alert procedures require two alternative plans; one to be followed when the disaster occurs during normal working hours, the other to be followed after hours and on weekends. The procedures should include a designation of alternates to provide for the possibility that the person charged with primary responsibility might be on vacation, attending an out-of-town meeting, or ill.

I. The Alert phase is the period immediately after notification that a disaster has occurred or is about to occur.

   A. Notify all those who may be involved in the assistance effort that their help may be required and that preliminary preparations should be started.

   B. Notify other offices and officials in the agency network of the event.

   C. Call staff together quickly to review plan.

   D. Include in the alert message the location of the disaster control center being established by the area agency.

   E. A feature of the control center will be a special information and referral service for elderly disaster victims. This should be a special number. With proper preparation, the regular I & R personnel can assume this function.

   F. Include in the alert phase the transporting of supplies and equipment for use in the center and for subsequent activities.

   G. Anticipate that the first requirement will be staff transportation. The alert notification is the signal for the responsible individuals to be sure that one or more autos are available, with full gas tanks.

   H. Initiate the calling of a list of appropriate individuals not on the AAA staff. This list would include the State Office of Aging, contractors who may be called on to provide certain services, caterers and site managers who would be expected to respond to food needs.

Assessment

II. The assessment phase includes those actions necessary to collect sufficient information to determine the type, scope, and location of area agency disaster assistance activities. These activities should be completed within twenty-four hours.

Psychologically, this is the most difficult part of the immediate response. The natural reaction to an emergency is to react, to do something even if it is not clear what the priorities for action should be. There will be pressure from all directions to have exact numbers of victims, locations of disaster impact, and a detailed account of activities of the area agency even before the dust has settled or the flooding created. Remember: respond; do not react.

A. Assess the impact of the disaster on the elderly:

1. Numbers of affected senior citizens. (Remember nursing homes populations; locations of all nursing homes in area should be noted, affected or not).

2. Special needs of the elderly (including the type of loss).

Often a disaster will result in side effects hazardous to health or safety. Floods and hurricanes many times produce polluted water supplies. Gas leaks, caused by broken mains, pose the danger of explosion. Any number of possible hazards to life are involved if industries and storage facilities are with the affected area.

The loss of utilities itself can become a major problem. Complete loss of electricity, gas, water, and telephone service can be expected within the major damage area; fringe areas can experience interruption of service. These services are needed for preparation of food and preservation of conditions essential for adequate shelter.

Contact power and water utility companies in assessing home damage and maintenance needs of the elderly.

3. Kinds of services needed and scarcity and disruption of transportation is often experienced by disaster areas. Bridges may be out and familiar roads may become unfamiliar and unpassable. Public transportation is frequently at a stand-

still in the damaged areas. Provision of emergency transportation becomes mandatory in the relocation of persons and in transporting injured to hospitals.

    4. Geographical scope of the disaster.

        a. Assess amount of damage inflicted on seniors. This should include what type of senior citizens (frail, low-income) are victims, and their potential short- and long-term needs.

        b. Assume the immediate assessments of services may not be precisely accurate and keep flexible in recognizing that new needs will arise.

        c. Assess the adequacy of services being delivered immediately following the disaster, be sensitive to gaps, and advocate where needed for additional services and resources.

        d. Report collected information as soon as possible. This should be provided directly to the State Office on Aging. The telephoned report should be followed by a written one.

B. Assess the impact on resources:

    1. Area Agency resources.

    2. Other community resources.

C. Basic methods of assessment.

    1. Radio and telephone monitoring.

    2. On-site.

    3. Obtaining information from other agencies.

    4. C B radio.

    5. Property tax rolls.

    6. Census information.

III. Action

The third phase is Action toward assistance. This begins as soon as there is sufficient information to indicate that a specific action is necessary. Action is a continuing phase, with the new actions initiated as new information is received and analyzed.

   A. Evacuation and relocation (temporary and permanent).

   Sometimes AAA personnel may be needed at this stage, particularly as an Advocate: contact Civil Defense, Red Cross.

   The action phase will proceed much more smoothly if the alert phase has been effective and the assessment realistic. Deploying planned resources is relatively simple compared to locating resources as needs develop. With a good assessment, the kinds of resources (services and funding) and the quantity will be known.

   Three priority services are almost always assessment of damages, advocate service, and legal services. Other priorities must then be set.

   B. Contact sheriff office personnel in rural areas to determine victims in need of assistance.

   C. Keep ongoing contact with state and regional AoA offices for consultation and guidance regarding assistance, resources and new apparent needs. In the case of a nationally declared disaster, pass the information on to the Federal Emergency Management.

   D. The mass media should be utilized to disseminate information on your agency's services and on insurance and contractors problems. Short, informative articles or public service presentations, frequently repeated, may be an effective means of increasing awareness of services, potential problems and frauds - as well as encouraging people to initiate recovery processes.

      1. In any disaster, information may be distorted. The AAA should create mechanisms such as rumor control and use its Information and Referral component to verify information. Only persons having clear authority should be heeded; AAA's should carefully check out sources of information to determine their validity.

2. Remember that the very persons who need services the most critically may be without electricity. Useful information on regular radio stations is more likely to be heard via the transistor radio.

3. Spread information through media and individual contacts. However, when the population is widely scattered, individual contact is the most effective method of information. Use your I & R component as a referral center.

E. Pinpoint sources to locate victims, such as mailmen (door-to-door), merchants, and churches which may be willing to supply a list of senior parishioners. Remember, in a disaster, people may move in with relatives and streets may lose their identity. Give churches information on your services; they can refer seniors to you.

F. Establish contact with desk clerks in order to reach occupants of singleroom-occupancy hotels.

G. Continue outreach activities long after the disaster. Efforts should be made to locate victims reluctant to seek aid or unaware that aid is available. The concept of "agressive casework" applies here.

H. If FEMA is involved, you and/or state agency will be reporting to them daily during disaster, and weekly for a period thereafter.

I. It should be remembered that in a Federally declared disaster, the usual restrictions on use of program resources would not apply. Any disaster relief services provided by the area agency would be made available for all victims, not just the elderly.

FISCAL

I. The urgency of a disaster response may prevent the use of established lines of authority and normal approval processes. It is imperative that the AAAs develop a system that will permit immediate funding action without loss of accountability.

II. When a disaster strikes, the Area Agency must immediately have access to the following information on funds:

   A. Funds of the AAA which are currently unobligated and can be shifted to meet the needs of disaster victims.

   B. If the above funds are insufficient to meet the needs, the AAA should ask the State Office of Aging if they have unobligated funds, or funds which could be diverted to the disaster victims.

   C. If the above funds are still insufficient, the State Office of Aging will request, through Regional Office, reimbursement cost up to $40,000 (incurred by the state) from Part C, Section 421.

   D. If all these funds are insufficient, Regional Office will request a mission assignment from FEMA for funds. (This source can only be used in a nationally declared disaster.)

III. To be able to allocate or reallocate funds of the AAA:

   A. Discuss with grantee organization or board the need for an expeditious mechanism of allocating or reallocating funds.

   B. Agree upon a system to be used.

   C. Revise bylaws to show approved procedure and person delegated the authority to act.

   D. Discuss with the State Office of Aging procedures for expediting plan revisions.

   E. Ask for written confirmation of procedure.

IV. Receipt and use of additional state/federal funds:

   A. Develop a procedure with the State Office of Aging for awarding additional funds. This system may include:

   1. Verbal approval followed by a telegram.

   2. Notification of grant award.

3. A grant application and plan revision to reflect the use of funds.

*All of the above are in the reverse order of standard operating procedures.

    B. Supporting documentation must be kept by AAA of expenditure of funds.

V. Receipt and use of Part C, Section 421 funds:

    A. The State Office of Aging will work out a grant application with the help of the Area Agency.

    B. The grant application will usually be teletyped to AoA.

    C. Notification of approval or disapproval will be teletyped back to Regional Office and called into the State (later the Notification of Grant Award will be mailed to the State Office).

    D. The state will instruct the Area Agency to obligate, based upon the prearranged procedure of the State and Area Agency.

    E. Supporting documentation must be kept by AAA of expenditure of funds.

VI. Receipt and use of FEMA funds:

    A. The Regional Office will verbally notify the State Office of Aging of "mission assignment" approval, (Notice will include purpose, funding ceiling). This will be followed by written confirmation to the State Office of Aging.

    B. The State Agency will advance funds necessary to the AAA for implementation of program by the agreed upon procedure. These funds will be reimbursed by FEMA.

    C. The Area Agency may be instructed to keep a special fiscal system for the accounting of these funds. This procedure will be outlined by the State or Regional Office.

PREPLANNING (BASIC COORDINATION AND INTEGRATION)

In order to be prepared, the area agency must develop a written disaster response plan. The plan should be practical and simple; however, it must be created so that the plan is comprehensive and relevant to the variety of disasters that potentially could hit the geographic area serviced by the area agency.

I. Considerations in developing a Disaster Response Plan:

   A. Consider the capabilities and limitation of the AAA.

   B. Consider conjunctions with other agencies.

   C. Consider the plans and responsibilities of AoA and and the state.

   D. Consider the extent of disaster planning in the AAA service area.

   E. Consider the roles of various relief agencies in the AAA service area.

   F. Consider the organizations primarily responsible for relief authority in each community.

   G. Consider, when working with large and diverse geographic area, subdividing into workable quadrants.

   H. Consider the types of disasters prevalent in the AAA service area, the relative probability of occurrence, magnitude, location, and effects on geographic areas (people, systems, facilities, resources, institutions).

   I. Consider plan for dissemination of information to other organizations who will be collecting data and doing needs assessment.

   J. Consider the necessity of the AAA to assume a greater degree of responsibility in non-national disasters (such as hotel fires and storms resulting in loss of utilities).

II. Coordination efforts:

   A. Investigate available disaster assistance and determine where gaps exist.

   B. Request inclusion in area disaster assistance planning efforts and if none exist, help initiate such efforts.

C. Assure that agencies involved in disaster assistance know what services and data the AAA can provide.

D. Provide an inventory of community resources for the elderly (especially that developed by Information and Referral) for input into community disaster systems.

E. View this planning process as an opportunity to educate emergency organizations to the special needs of the elderly.

F. Establish a working relationship and where appropriate written agreements with area organizations.

G. Identify data needed from other agencies when gathering victim information. Working agreements would be helpful. For example, many agencies do not list age of victim, only the need.

III. Compile a standard operational procedure, outlining response process when a disaster is reported.

A. Define duties and responsibilities.

B. Determine alerting procedures for both working and non-working hours.

C. Determine procedures when communications are affected.

D. Locate operation centers and alternates when primary center is in affected area.

E. Determine policies for personnel and allowable expenses.

F. Determine procedures for obligation/responsibility regarding non-presidentially declared disaster (or before the presidential disaster is declared).

IV. Immediately after a disaster the AAA will be asked to identify the number of elderly affected by the disaster. Information which will facilitate identification should be obtained in advance and incorporated into the disaster plan. To clearly identify the victims, the AAA should collect all pertinent information in an easily understood directory. This material should be available for disaster related organizations. In addition to organization and community contacts (see Appendix), the AAA should collect information from the following resources:

A. Compile voter registration lists.

B. Compile property tax exemption lists.

C. Compile the latest census information on the number of seniors by county or track and block-group.

- D. Design maps that pinpoint heavy concentrations of elderly people (particularly institutionalized elderly).

- E. Design maps of concentrations of one person senior households.

- F. Identify concentrations of low income, minority, and ethnic groups, especially those who do not speak English and would need an interpreter.

- G. Identify locations of apartment dwellers whose need might go unanswered because of their solitude. Apartment dwellers often move immediately after a disaster.

- H. Identify locations of home owners.

- I. Compile socio-economic characteristics of the seniors; class differences may point out differing needs. Often lower socio-economic individuals lack the insurance and need more assistance than upper and middle classes.

- J. Identify locations of nursing homes and high rise apartments; consider the special needs of these residences. For example, planners should have some idea of the number of non-ambulatory persons living in nursing homes.

- K. Remember the "grapevine technique."

    1. Individuals who know the community and the elderly residents.

    2. Door-to-door mailmen.

    3. Grocery markets with home delivery.

    4. Church groups that visit "shut-ins."

    5. Desk clerks of single occupancy hotels.

V. Communications.

- A. Major problems in past disasters have been inadequate establishment and maintence of good communications.

    1. Horizonal - within affected community.

    2. Vertical - within aging structure.

B. AAA should inform state agency.

   1. Data gathered which establishes disaster impact on elderly.

   2. Actions to be initiated.

C. Often reporting/communications appear extraneous to overburdened AAA staff, but consciencious performance will enable network representative to:

   1. Keep others informed, thus avoiding additional inquiries,

   2. Make appropriate decisions,

   3. Access additional resources; and,

   4. Perform institutional advocacy.

D. AAA should attend or receive report of daily debriefing sessions conducted by FEMA.

E. Purpose of FEMA meeting.

   1. Information exchanged by disaster agencies.

   2. Concerns exchanged by disaster agencies.

   3. Interagency planning efforts.

   4. Interagency coordination efforts.

F. AAA should establish set pattern for staff debriefings.

   1. Sessions should include Disaster Advocates (even if outposted in distant parts of PSA).

   2. May need to be conducted daily.

   3. Excellent means of training new staff.

   4. Must be conducted at least weekly.

G. Without AAA staff debriefings, erroneous assumptions will develop resulting in hardships for the elderly.

H. Standardized format has been utilized in recent disasters. (See attachment)

   1. AAA's tend to ignore or limit attention to narrative section.

2. Statistics tell very little of actual situation encountered.

3. Narrative useful in assuring successes/difficulties are understood.

4. Narrative documents situation so appropriate action can be taken.

VI. As AAA returns to normalcy, less attention to disaster response/return to programmatics.

1. Watch for timelags which create unnecessary new problems for elderly.

2. Ignored narrative reports can result in disservice for older persons.

SUPPLIES

I. The AAA should prepare and store duplicate necessary supplie in more than one location (this is a precautionary measure should the storage location be inaccessible).

II. The minimum supplies should include:

   A. Identification supplies.

   1. Lapel badges or arm bands for staff and volunteers.

   2. Cards for vehicle identification.

   B. Form and record supplies.

   1. Forms (see sample in appendix) for records of contacts and action taken.

   2. Forms to record telephone calls received and replies.

   3. Forms for recording time of temporary employees.

   4. Forms for travel expense reimbursement.

   C. Contact sources

   1. Printed list of volunteers home and work telephone numbers.

   2. Printed list of administration, office staff, and field staff's home and work telephone numbers.

   3. Printed list of agencies (including State and Regional Office of Aging).

   D. Office supplies.

   1. Legal pads.

   2. Pens.

   3. Pencils.

   4. Stapler.

   5. Staples.

   6. Index cards.

   7. Paper clips.

   8. Masking tape.

9. Scotch tape.

10. Scissors.

11. Flashlight and batteries.

E. Public Information.

1. Brochures or leaflets on the services provided by the area agency. Be sure that publications include a telephone number and contact person.

2. Mass media should be utilized by public service announcements or display ads, if necessary.

    a. Information on the access of services provided by the area agency should be disseminated.

    b. Information related to potential problems and detection of frauds should be disseminated.

3. AAA's comprehensive disaster preparedness plan should be disseminated to agencies with whom contacts have been established.

TRAINING

I. Considerations during planning process:

   A. Evaluate and consider including disaster preparedness training provided by other agencies.

   B. Invite representation from other agencies to the in-house disaster preparedness training.

      1. Will provide other agencies with an awareness of the AAA role in Disaster Preparedness.

      2. Will allow the AAA to educate other agencies to the special needs of the elderly during a crisis.

II. Should prepare a Disaster Preparedness Training Package.

III. Should provide technical assistance to nutrition sites and senior centers in drafting local disaster procedures.

IV. Should provide Disaster Preparedness Training on a regular basis.

   A. Must conduct disaster preparedness training for aging network. In addition to administrative, office and field staff, volunteers and aging boards should be included.

   B. Consider sending appropriate staff to assist companion AAA's if they should experience a disaster. (Experience is a sound educational device).

   C. Should encourage staff to utilize other agency's disaster training programs.

   D. Should provide special training concerning zoning codes, building codes, contracts, interviewing skills, and regulations concerning mechanics liens.

   E. Should establish a disaster education program for the elderly.

      1. Should conduct training sessions in places frequented by senior citizens.

      2. Should conduct training on a regular basis so that it will accommodate participant changes.

      3. Should address language related to disasters (for example, distinguish between "watches" and "warnings") in training session.

      4. Should address precautionary measures in training sessions.

5. Should include warning response drills and/or demonstrations in training sessions.

6. Should evaluate training effectiveness.

   a. Should share with other disaster relief agencies results of evaluation.

   b. Should resolve problems determined by evaluation process.

G. Should simulate a disaster as a training exercise. Drills are as successful as the effort by the planners and the degree of realism that can be obtained.

1. Should give particular attention to communications. The effectiveness of the AAA staff, volunteers, community, and organizational reporting system should be evaluated.

2. Should evaluate total impact of disaster preparedness training.

SERVICES

Arrange for Services in Advance

In planning for needed services, assume that no other agency will be prepared to meet all of the special needs of the elderly.

It is important to note that in a disaster the area agency services and programs can become community resources and the area agency staff should take a flexible (non-provincial) perspective.

I. Considerations in preplanning for services:

   A. Consider that additional services may be required if disaster should occur at the end of the month. Elderly at this time of month will be short of funds, perhaps low on prescriptions and food.

   B. Many disaster experiences show that the elderly, many of whom have never been the recipient of any agency services are extremely reluctant to accept services or even acknowledge their need, as this service is viewed as charity. An educational program will need to be developed.

   C. Many elderly will resist being moved from their home even though it is hazardous. Special counseling and follow-ups will be needed.

   D. Special attention will need to be given to frail elderly in moving or relocating to new housing.

   E. Special efforts will be needed to contact the hard to reach elderly and incorporate them into the service delivery system.

II. Types of services needed. (See Services)

   A. Certain services are almost mandated in any type of disaster affecting the elderly. Those services have been identified as the following:

      1. Transportation services,

      2. Legal services,

      3. Independent housing professional appraisal services

      4. Elderly advocacy services. Advocacy, when applied to the elderly in a disaster, can be a type of careful guidance of the older persons through the maze of services available after the devastation

B. Much of the direct or sub-contracted services which can be offered by the agency employing already existing resources such as the following:

1. Counseling and advocacy,
2. Information and referral,
3. Home delivered meals and centralized nutrition sites,
4. Senior centers,
5. Legal assistance,
6. USDA foods as food bank,
7. Transportation,
8. Health clinics,
9. Chore service for debris removal,
10. Homemaker,
11. Home handyman assistance, and
12. Volunteers (RSVP, Friendly Visitors, etc.)

III. AAA planning for needed services.

A. Should have a prearranged contract/agreement with an attorney or Legal Aid Office for services during a disaster.

B. Should prearrange for the services of an independent appraiser so that a telephone call will elicit an immediate response.

C. Should have a listing of reputable, well-known local contractors to be used for consultation and estimates.

D. Should familiarize themselves with the process of insurance adjustments and claims processing. (See Training)

E. Should insert a clause in all subcontracts which provides for additional services at the time of a disaster.

F. Should plan for the continuation of present services which may require the relocation of nutrition programs, relocation of health clinics, or replacement of vehicles used for transportation.

- G. Should develop a listing of area agencies on aging's resources in other parts of the state which could be mobilized to assist victims (for example: buses, food, counselors, and specialized professionals.)

- H. Should identify individuals knowledgeable concerning local zoning codes and local permits. These persons can respond to serious concerns about rebuilding.

IV. How to notify the elderly of available services.

- A. Should use the existing agencies in the community as well as the assigned disaster relief agencies.

- B. The AAA should disseminate a pamphlet telling senior citizens of AAA services and identify contact persons. These could be disseminated in door to door needs assessment, left in local grocery stores, distributed during Sunday church services.

- C. Should use Information and Referral component as a referral center.

- D. Should employ Outreach maximizing resources and contacts to assure that the elderly are both aware of services available and encouraged to seek assistance, as needed.

- F. Should provide a mechanism for determining length of service provision. (See Appendix)

INDEPENDENT APPRAISER SERVICE

I. Contract should be in place prior to disaster, if possible.

II. Should be one of the first persons brought to disaster scene.

III. Purpose of appraiser's service.

   A. Victims often confronted with losses not covered through existing insurance policies.

   B. Victims question appropriateness of insurance settlements.

   C. Victims require loss varification for grant applications.

IV. Advantages of having appraiser service.

   A. Able to bring expertise, insight.

   B. Able to bring objectivity to victim and insurance adjuster who is trying to save company money.

   C. Able to reassure victims.

   D. Able to give victims confidence that AAA is assisting.

      1. Individual not left to own devices to determine loss.

      2. Individual not left to own devices to challenge decisions.

   E. Able to better substantiate applications for Small Business Administration loans.

   F. Able to better substantiate applications for Family Assistance grants.

   G. Able to assist in appealing decisions.

   H. Able to provide valid information to advocates and legal service.

V. Expense incurred in securing independent appraisal is minimum compared to benefits.

   A. Able to assure equitable settlements.

   B. Able to minimize stressful situations.

VI. Long-term service.

ADVOCACY

I. Core service which encourages delivery of services to elderly victims.

II. Most visible respresentative of AAA in disaster relief.

III. Usually employed during stressful time.

IV. Help elderly become aware of programs and services.

    A. Disaster relief agencies.

    B. AAA.

V. Responsibilities.

    A. Develops knowledge of various relief programs.

    B. Interviews victims.

    C. Assess needs.

    D. Reassures individuals experiencing crisis.

    E. Provides emotional support.

    F. Determines best resource for meeting needs.

    G. Identifies persons with needs beyond scope of offered programs.

    H. Assists in rebuilding, returning to normalcy.

    I. Develops trusting relationship with victim.

    J. Assists elderly at disaster center.

    K. Links victims with services after disaster center closed.

    L. Negotiates decisions, assists victim in appeals process if relief programs issue a denial.

    M. Provides inter-agency information.

    N. Provides information for public.

VI. Abilities required.

    A. Be able to relate well with people.

    B. Be a good listener.

- C. Be aware of special problems faced by disaster victims.
- D. Be aware of client shock reaction.
- E. Be knowledgeable of programs and services available.

VII. Long-term service.
- A. Responds/refers inquiries about assistance months after original impact.
- B. Whether designated staff or sole purpose employee AAA's have found need to retain for extended periods of time.

LEGAL SERVICES

I. Typical needs.

   A. Problems with insurance settlements.

   B. Problems with bureaucratic decisions.

   C. Appeals on grant applications.

   D. Appeals on SBA loan applications.

   E. Problems with property title opinions.

   F. Protection from persons who take advantage of victim's vulnerability.

   G. Problems with building/repair firms (i.e., quality of service).

II. Legal Services should be available immediately.

   A. Through contracted attorney, or

   B. Through cooperation with bar associations (Young Lawyers Section of many bar associations provide assistance for disaster centers).

III. Attorneys working at a disaster center should <u>not</u> take cases that will be fee producing.

IV. Attorney can make officials aware of situations requiring change.

   A. Laws.

   B. Regulations.

   C. For example, zoning laws may not allow placement of temporary units but victim needs special permission for mobile home because damage caused home to be uninhabitable.

V. Advocates refer special problems to attorney.

   A. Representation at appeal's hearing.

   B. Negotiating contracts.

VI. Settlement resolution may be lengthy.

TRANSPORTATION

I. During disaster, elderly faced with immediate and long-term transportation needs.

II. AAA should recognize the limitations to access various forms of transportation (i.e., boats during floods).

III. With appropriate planning available vehicles can be maximized.

   A. Transportation system may be damaged or impaired.

   B. Need is intensified.

IV. During the emergency phase, transportation should be made available to all citizens.

V. Elderly victims should receive priority.

VI. AAA should include required disaster response in transportation contracts.

VII. Transportation request may be varied and tax AAA resources.

   A. Damaged nursing homes/senior citizen housing complexes may require transportation for resident relocation.

   B. Transportation may be needed for removing victims and belongings from hazardous locations.

   C. Request for medical/pharmaceutical transportation services will increase.

   D. Additional requests will occur for the following:

      1. Disaster Centers.

      2. Nutrition sites.

      3. Shopping assistance.

      4. Escort service.

      5. Home-delivered meals.

      6. Medical.

         a. Doctor.

         b. Pharmacy.

      E. Staff should be educated to victim's fear of leaving home and possessions for needed services.

         1. Fear home will be robbed or vandalized.

         2. Fear they will lose possessions.

VIII. Means for expanding service.

      A. Additional staff.

      B. Additional vehicles.

      C. Additional routes.

IX. Long-term service.

HOMEMAKER/CHORE SERVICE

I. Service provided through AAA.

II. Provides gap-filling service at time of disaster.

    A. Many volunteer organizations provide competent and cost-free assistance in debris removal, home repair and clean-up.

        1. But, not prepared for long-term services.

        2. But, assistance not accepted because persons are unfamiliar.

        3. But, do not have personnel adequate to serve all people with needs.

        4. But, appropriately go to areas where greatest amount of damage has been sustained.

        5. But, are not always aware of disasters of lesser impact.

    B. AAA Homemaker/Chore Service's help is required in restoring homes to order.

III. Service should be available for long-terms.

HANDIMAN SERVICES

I. Provided to a great degree by volunteer groups such as Mennonites (with AAA assisting with materials).

II. Need may exist long after emergency phase has passed.

III. Typical handiman needs.

    A. Repairing broken windows.

    B. Repairing furnaces.

    C. Repairing water heaters.

    D. Repairing steps.

    E. Making minor roof repairs.

    F. Pumping and cleaning flooded basements.

    G. Disinfecting.

    H. General cleaning.

IV. Services can either be provided directly by AAA through own employees or contracted with independent service provider.

V. Monitoring tools are required to insure repairs are satisfactorily completed.

    A. May be simple signature of approval.

    B. May be elaborate checklist.

VI. Disaster advocate should provide follow-up on client receiving handiman service.

OUTREACH

I. Persons not aware of available services need information.

II. Outreach efforts include:

   A. Brochures.

   B. Fliers.

   C. Public speeches.

   D. Public service announcements (media).

   E. Newspaper display and classified ads.

   F. Door-to-door mailmen.

   G. Church bulletins.

   H. Door-to-door canvassing.

III. Long-term service, requests continue sometimes months after Disaster Center has closed.

MEALS PROGRAM

I. Destroyed or uninhabital homes leave victims without means to provide personal meals.

II. Typical services include:

    A. Additional meals.

    B. Expanding facilities.

    C. Expanding hours.

III. Long-term service.

LONG-TERM SERVICES

I. Service needs exist long after disaster's initial impact.

   A. Often recovery, long slow process.

   B. Elderly victim suffers hardest disaster effects.

   C. Unique characteristics of elderly necessitates service continue for months.

II. Determining long-term needs by AAA.

   A. Flexibility must be stressed.

   B. Through recovery process, needs change.

   C. Adjust services to fit needs.

III. AAA response depends on type of disaster.

IV. Common ways Region VII has responded to long-term needs.

   A. Expanded existing services; such as

      1. Meals programs.

      2. Transportation.

      3. Outreach.

      4. Legal services.

      5. Handiman.

      6. Homemaker/Chore

   B. Provided special services, such as

      1. Disaster coordinators.

      2. Advocates.

      3. Independent appraisers.

PERSONNEL

I. Disaster Preparedness Coordinator.

   A. Critical step in equipping AAA toward addressing disaster situations.

   B. Person's efficiency determines success of recovery efforts.

   C. Qualities needed for Disaster Preparedness Coordinator:

   1. Should be able to immediately respond to potentially critical circumstances.

   2. Should accept responsibility for preparing AAA staff for role in relief and recovery efforts.

   3. Should be full-time staff member with professional responsibilities.

   4. Should be familiar with available services in PSA.

   5. Should be able to relate, train, and direct disaster advocates.

   6. Should be responsible for assuring AAA will provide assistance in a disaster situation.

   7. Should be responsible for assuring the sub-grantee contracts and grants are negotiated to provide assistance in a disaster situation.

   8. Should be responsible for working with volunteer network toward providing disaster assistance and relief activities.

   9. Should assist Federal agencies by providing review and comment on services and activities relative to disaster preparedness and response.

   10. Should determine goals and arrange training, conduct exercises, critique, and evaluate preparedness responses.

II. Considerations during the personnel planning process:

   A. The AAA should designate an individual as the Disaster Relief Coordinator.

   B. Employees are expected to assist in AAA relief efforts regardless of normal working hours.

C. If a national disaster is declared, personnel must staff the disaster center the total time that it is operational (this may be 12 hours a day, 7 days a week).

D. If the disaster is widespread, several disaster centers may be opened.

E. The AAA must consider methods of continuing every-day operations while personnel is working on disaster relief.

III. Developing personnel section of disaster plan.

A. Personnel policies should reflect that all employees are expected to work additional hours as needed during a disaster.

B. Personnel policies should explain how overtime will be handled.

C. Staff assignments should be prepared for all area agency staff. The disaster function should be incorporated into individual job descriptions.

D. Staff from subgrantee agencies should be assured by making this a part of the contract and a provision of the notification of grant award.

E. Gaps in area agency's skills and expertise should be identified (for example, a special counselor or advocate coordinator might be added to the core specialist staff in the event of a disaster).

F. Potential volunteers (include specialties and skills) should be listed in the plan.

G. When possible, volunteer assignments should be made on a geographic basis by blocks or block groups. This will minimize travel time, effort, and help maintain continuity in client-assistant (advocate) relationships.

H. Home phone numbers (as well as work numbers) of all staff and volunteers should be listed in plan. Directory assistance during disaster is not readily available.

I. Personnel and volunteer listings should be updated due to staffing changes and level of expertise changes.

IV. Personnel to keep normal work flowing. Work with Regional, State, and Area Agencies to develop a "cadre of disaster expertise." This cadre would serve as a resource to the area during both planning for disaster preparedness and during a real disaster. The cadre would free other staff members to proceed with their normal daily activities.

DISASTER ASSISTANCE CENTER

Overview

Federal Disaster Assistance Centers are established by the Federal Emergency Management Administration a few days after a disaster declaration has been made by the President of the United States. The center is established in one or more temporary locations. All federal agencies involved in disaster assistance will have representatives at the center. This includes Housing and Urban Development, Small Business Administration, Internal Revenue Service, Department of Agriculture, Veteran's Administration and the Administration on Aging. The state agencies responsible for Social Security programs and for food stamps, private agencies such as the American Red Cross and the Salvation Army, and various other organizations active in disaster response may also be represented. The centers are usually managed by Vista volunteers who are responsible for housekeeping details.

When disaster victims enter a center, the receptionist sends them to an intake interviewer who obtains the basic information on the victims' names, addresses, extent of damage, etc. The victims receive copies of the intake form which indicates the agencies the victims should contact. The victims then go to the representatives of these agencies, one after another, for the specific kind of assistance that could be provided by each agency, completing any necessary applications. Where any additional meetings with an agency are necessitated, or where a representative of an agency must inspect the damage before decision on an application for assistance can be reached, arrangements are made during this initial interview.

After visiting all representatives indicated on the intake form, the victims go to the exit interviewer who checks to see that all appropriate agencies have been visited, and that the victims are satisfied that the problems caused by the disaster have been addressed.

DISASTER ASSISTANCE CENTER

The victim, as indicated by the arrows, did not need Salvation Army or IRS assistance (according to the Intake Interviewer's analysis).

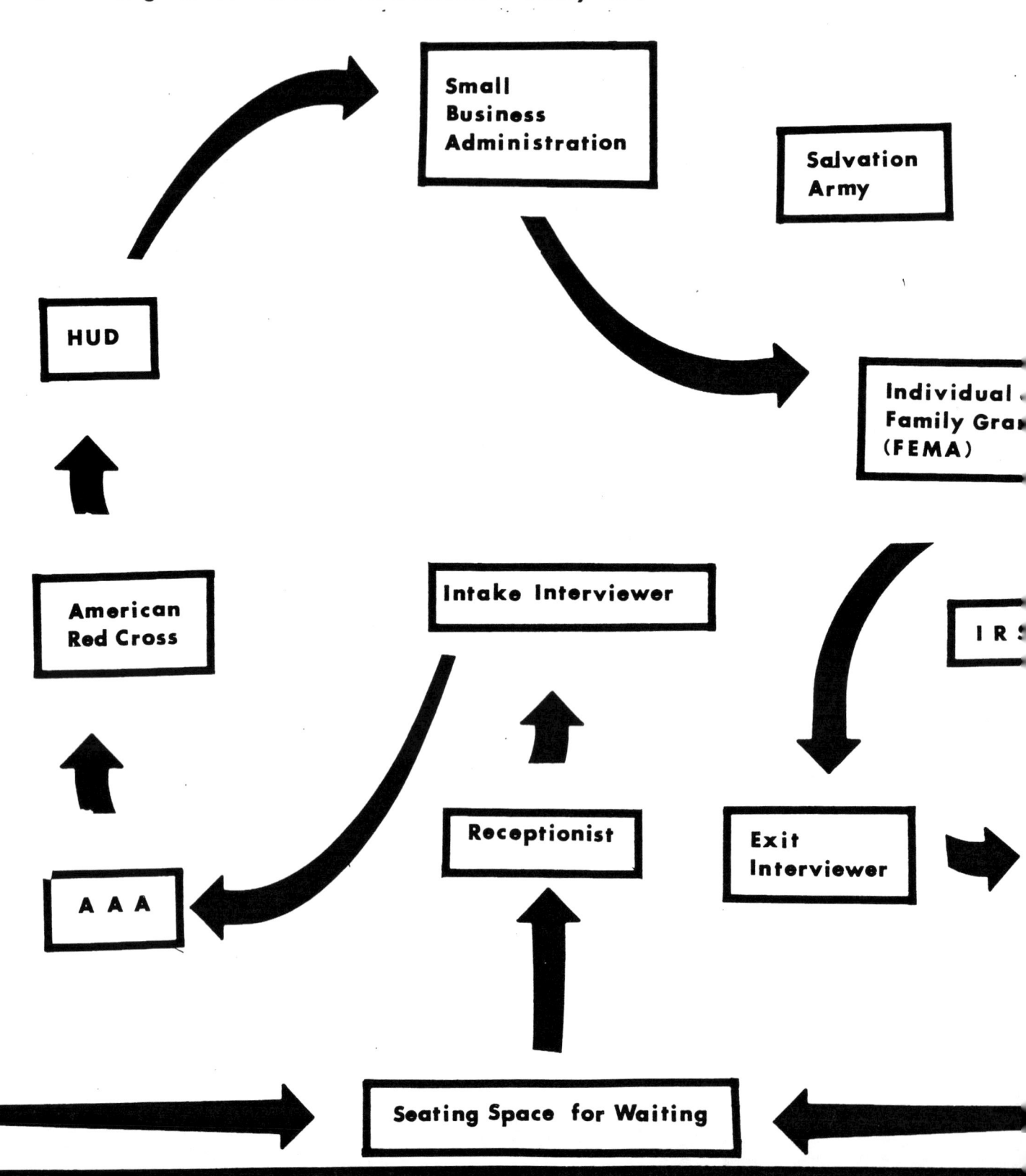

- Small Business Administration
- Salvation Army
- HUD
- Individual & Family Grant (FEMA)
- American Red Cross
- Intake Interviewer
- IRS
- AAA
- Receptionist
- Exit Interviewer
- Seating Space for Waiting

AAA Role

The Administration of Aging is represented at the Federal Disaster Assistance Center by the staff of the local Area Agency on Aging. The role of the area agency is not quite the same as that of other agencies. The primary function of the area agency is to assist the elderly victims who are going through the center. This involves first making the representatives of other agencies aware of some of the special problems older persons often have during and after a disaster, and second accompanying the elderly through the center. Of course like the other agencies the Area Agency on Aging will also interview elderly victims as regards services that it can provide.

More specifically, the area agency role in staffing Federal Disaster Assistance Centers should include the following:

1. <u>Personnel</u> to staff the desk maintained by the Area Agency at the center.

    There should be at least four AAA representatives on duty at a center at any one time. Since the centers may be open as long as ten or twelve hours a day, two or more shifts will be necessary.

    The ideal staffing pattern would include: (1) a social worker experienced in working with the elderly, who is familiar with the functioning of the existing social services structure, and who can solve the unusual problems that are sure to occur. (2) One or two community residents who know the elderly and who are known by them. (3) One or more individuals skilled in working with and assisting the elderly. Homemaker aides, nutrition site personnel, senior center staff will probably have the kind of experience needed for the task.

    If additional help can be obtained and if the center staff is agreeable, it is extremely helpful to have Area Agency personnel conducting the intake interview for elderly victims.

2. <u>Supplies</u>.

    In operating the center desk, the personnel will need the following supplies:

    A. Identification badges giving the name of the Area Agency and the name of the individual.

    B. Information blanks to obtain basic information for follow-up activities.

    C. Legal pads, pens, pencils, stapler, paper clips.

D. Brochures for the elderly describing the function of the Area Agency on disaster.

E. Brochures or leaflets on the other services provided by the Area Agency that would be most helpful to disaster victims.

F. Phone numbers of the agencies that disaster center staff might need to contact.

3. <u>What To Do</u>

The staff assigned to the center should be at the center at least a half-hour before opening time. During this period, the staff should establish some contact with other agencies, explaining the role of the area agency, and finding out what each of the other agencies will be doing.

When the center opens, it should be made clear to the intake workers that elderly are to be referred to the AAA station. One staff member should go up to the elderly person, explain what the AAA will be doing, and take the elderly individual first to the intake interviewer, then to the appropriate agency. If the elderly person needs to be escorted from agency to agency, the AAA will be prepared to do so.

If possible arrange for representatives of the other agencies to come to the more infirm elderly, rather than require the elderly to wait in several lines.

Explain to the elderly that the area agency personnel will be contacting them again to see if their problems are being solved, and will help if needed in obtaining any additional action from other agencies after the centers are closed.

Transportation to and from the disaster center will probably be a major problem. The area agency may be the only source for this service, using the vehicles normally used in Title III or Title VII programs. Providing this transportation service is, in addition to serving an urgent need, extremely helpful in establishing credibility with victims and with other agencies.

Resources Available from Selected Disaster Relief Agencies*

TEMPORARY HOUSING

Purpose of Assistance - To provide temporary housing for individuals and families displaced as a result of a disaster.

Provided by - Department of Housing and Urban Development following a Presidential Declaration of a major disaster or an emergency.

Assistance Available - Living kits and furniture. Temporary housing in the form of government, private and commercial resources or minimal repair to owner-occupied damaged structures is provided. Temporary housing may be provided, rent-free, for up to 12 months, dependent upon need.

Eligible Applicants - Individuals and families displaced from their homes by a disaster.

Application Procedure - Application is made through the local HUD Disaster Field or Sub-Office.

Information Source - Regional Office of the Federal Disaster Assistance Administration (See Appendix for addresses)
or
Emergency Preparedness Staff
Department HUD
451 - 7th Street, S. W., Room 9132
Washington, D. C. 20410
or
Federal Disaster Assistance Administration
Department of Housing and Urban Development
Washington, D. C. 20410

Authorization - The Disaster Relief Act of 1974, Public Law 93-288, 88 Stat. 143, Section 404; Executive Order 11795

---

* Abstracted from the Digest of Federal Disaster Assistance U.S. Department of Housing and Urban Development, Federal Disaster Assistance Administration.

LEGAL SERVICES

Purpose of Assistance - To provide assistance to low-income individuals who require a legal service as a result of a major disaster.

Provided by - Appropriate Federal Agencies, State and local bar associations and the Young Lawyers Section of the American Bar Association following a Presidential declaration of a major disaster.

Information Source - Regional offices of the Emergencies Management Administration (See Appendix for addresses)
or
Federal Disaster Assistance Administration
Department of Housing and Urban Development
Washington, D.C. 20410

Authorization - Disaster Relief Act of 1974, Public Law 93-288, 88Stat. 143, Section 412; Executive Order 11795.

EMERGENCY FOOD STAMP PROGRAM

Purpose of Assistance - Free food stamps to insure that adequate amounts of nutritious food are available for disaster victims.

Provided by - U.S. Department of Agriculture (Food and Nutrition Service), following national level approval by the Assistant Secretary for Marketing and Consumer Services.

Information Source - Food and Nutrition Service
U.S. Department of Agriculture
Washington, D.C. 20250
or
Federal Emergency Management
Department of Housing and Urban Development
Washington, D.C. 20410

Authorization - Disaster Relief Act of 1974, Public Law 93-288, Section 409; Executive Order 11795; Food Stamp Act of 1964, as amended

AMERICAN NATIONAL RED CROSS

Purpose of Assistance - To provide food, clothing, shelter, first aid, supplementary nursing, hospital care, and blood products distributed to shelters, aid and feeding stations, or to individual families.

Provided by - American National Red Cross.

Information Source - Local Red Cross Chapter
or
American National Red Cross
Washington, D.C. 20006

Authorization - Act of January 5, 1905, as amended; Disaster Relief Act of 1974, Public Law 93-288; Executive Order 11795.

MENNONITE DISASTER SERVICE

Purpose of Assistance - To assist individuals and communities in repair and rehabilitation work following a disaster.

Provided by - The Mennonite Disaster Service.

Information Source - The Mennonite Disaster Service
21 South 12th Street
Akron, Pennsylvania 17501

Authorization - Not established by Federal Law, but recognized as a disaster relief organization by the Disaster Relief Act of 1974, Public Law 93-288.

TAX INFORMATION

Purpose of Assistance - To ensure that taxpayers, suffering losses as a result of a major disaster or emergency, receive the most current information regarding casualty loss claims, amended tax returns, and late filing of tax returns.

Provided by - Internal Revenue Service.

Information Source - Nearest Internal Revenue Service Office
or
Director, Training Division
Internal Revenue Service
Washington, D.C.

Authorization - Internal Revenue Code as amended.

UNEMPLOYMENT ASSISTANCE

Purpose of Assistance- To provide financial assistance to persons unemployed as a result of a major disaster.

Provided by - Department of Labor following a Presidential declaration of a major disaster.

Information Source - State Employment Agency
or
Department of Labor
Washington, D.C. 20210

Authorization - Disaster Relief Act of 1974, Public Law 93-288, Section 407: Executive Order 11795.

HOME REPAIR LOANS

Purpose of Assistance- To provide loan assistance for the refinancing repair, rehabilitation, or replacement of property damaged as a result of a natural disaster.

Provided by - The Small Business Administration, either with a Presidential declaration of a major disaster or a declaration by the Administration of SBA.

Information Source - Local or Regional Office of Small Business Administration
or
Office of Disaster Operations
Small Business Administration
1441 L Street, N.W.
Washington, D.C. 20416

Authorization - Small Business Act, as amended, Section 7 (b) (1), Public Law 85-536, as amended; Disaster Relief Act of 1970 Public Law 91-606, as amended, Sections 231, 234, and 235; Public Law 93-24.

THE SALVATION ARMY

Purpose of Assistance- Multiple services meet the needs of victims of natural and man-made disaster

Provided by - The Salvation Army.

Information Source - The Salvation Army, National Public
Affairs Office,
1001 - 14th Street, N.W.
Washington, D.C. 20005

Authorization - The Salvation Army Charter, May 12,
1899; The Disaster Relief Act of 1974,
Public Law 93-288.

INDIVIDUAL AND FAMILY GRANTS

Purpose of Assistance- To provide grants to meet disaster-
related necessary expenses or serious
needs of individuals or families
adversely affected by a major disaster.

Provided by - The state following a Presidential
declaration of a major disaster and
a request by the Governor to the
Federal Emergency Management Administration that the grant program be imple-
mented. (The program is funded by
a 75/25 Federal/State cost sharing).

Information Source - State Disaster Office
or
Federal Disaster Assistance Administration
Department of Housing and Urban Development
Washington, D.C. 20410

Authorization - Disaster Relief Act of 1974, 88 Stat. 143,
Section 408, Executive Order 11795.

Appendix·1

Aspects of Disaster Response Peculiar to Specific Categories of Disasters

AGRICULTURAL

This involves a major crop loss over the affected area and may be the result of natural or man-made plant destroying substance. Elements of an agricultural disaster may accompany other disasters listed here.

    Lead time: Variable; from almost none to months or years.
    Damage   : Extensive to flora in area.
    Casulties: Usually slight unless the cause is a man-made toxic substance.
    Primary/ : Foremost initial action should be cooperation
    Long term with relevant agencies in disseminating
    Action   information about the disasters causing agents; follow up activity may include loan and even relocation advocacy.

BLIZZARD

A severe snow storm accompanied by very high winds. In coastal areas this may lead to dangerously high tides and danger of local flooding.

    Lead time: In most cases several hours at most.
    Damage   : Initial damage will be from winds and tides which can cause serious structural damage. Long range effects from drifting and thawing, or from flooding, will be similar to that under FLOODS.
    Casulties: Can be severe in damaged areas. Also a need to be alert for possible starvation or freezing situations due to disruption of transportation and supply capabilities.
    Primary/ : As mentioned above, telephone, electricity
    Long term and supply resources may be curtailed
    Action   and the elderly are particularly susceptible to the problems of isolation engendered by these circumstances. Emergency food, power, and medical services may have to be established. In the long run the usual advocacy procedures for damage collection will have to be instituted.

EARTHQUAKE

Severe seismic disturbances that may be localized or generalized.

- Lead time: The state of the art at present still only allows for several hours real warning at best.
- Damage : Extensive in the affected area. Even more serious are the secondary effects caused by the initial tremors; these include widespread fires, local flooding due to ruptured water mains, and the possible escape of toxic substances from damaged containers.
- Casulties: Heavy in affected areas from both the tremors and the secondary effects.
- Primary/ Long term Action : Providing emergency services of all kinds for those in the affected area. Long range activity will run the gamut of all possible advocacy services including rebuilding or even relocating.

EPIDEMIC

Widescale medical emergency.

- Lead time: None at first, afterwards self-sustaining for duration of emergency.
- Damage : Nil, unless possible contamination forces razing of buildings.
- Casulties: Depending on the particular emergency this could range from slight to total It should always be borne in mind, however, that the elderly are often more susceptible to medical problems and that their needs in this area are often greater than that for the general public.
- Long term/ Primary Action: This will mainly involve making sure the elderly are appraised of the on-going medical emergency and seeing that their special needs and wants are not lost in the shuffle. Long term activity should be minimal.

FIRE (Area wide)

A large scale fire emergency that could arise from another emergency (i.e. EARTHQUAKE) or from a widespread forest or prairie fire.

- Lead time: Once detected it should be hours or days.

Damage	: Very severe. It should be kept in mind that flood damage may be very tricky to evaluate and objects that appear structually sound may have been ruined anyway by water that later receeded. An example would be a furnace whose malfunctioning might not be seen until months later. Thus, damage claim advocacy must be wide ranging.
Casulties:	Depending on the lead time, these could range from slight to severe.
Primary/ Long term Action	: The most immediate need is to assist in rescue and evacuation, identifying areas where there may be elderly people in need of assistance. Long range elderly people in need of assistance. Long range services will include assisting in damage claims, helping to obtain home repair loans and the like.

HEAT WAVE

A prolonged period of abnormally high temperatures, ofter accompanied by the effects of POLLUTION.

Lead time:	Self-generating.
Damage	: Nil.
Casulties:	The death rate among the elderly rises sharply during any sustained heat wave, especially among those with respiratory difficulties but preventive action can eliminate these heat related deaths.
Primary/ Long term Action	: This will largely involve establishing temporary facilities for those among the elderly whose normal living conditions would create an hazardous environment during a heat wave, and making these facilities known to the area elderly.

HURRICANE

A severe tropical storm that carries with it high winds and heavy rains. The combination of both can cause dangerous flooding in coastal and watershed areas.

Lead time:	Generally a few hours, at least, but the path of a hurricane is very unpredictable, as is its strength and a seemingly spent storm that is well out to sea may suddenly veer in direction and pick up strength as it procedes.

Damage   : Great, both from winds and flooding.
                 (See FLOOD for special damage assessment procedures)
Casulties: Moderate to great, depending on the strength of the storm and its secondary effects, such as flooding.
Primary/   :   Generally similar to FLOOD. Evacuation
Long term   and rescue in the immediate stages fol-
Action   lowed by wide ranging advocacy activities.

NUCLEAR

This will usually mean a peace time nuclear disaster and could involve either an explosion, followed by the effects of radiation or the escape of radioactive particles into the air.

Lead time: None.
Damage   :   Near total after an explosion; simple particle release will be akin to POISON.
Casulties: Likely to be very great, coupled with the after effects of radiation poisoning.
Primary/ :   Iniatially this will involve any assistance
Long term   that might be given in rescue operations.
Action   One thing that is sure is that any disaster resulting from a nuclear emergency will result in an immediate and total federal response so that aside from taking any normal disaster emergency steps local groups will probably be given directions from federal disaster units anyway.

POISON

Localized or widespread escape of toxic substances from any of a lengthy list of possible sources.

Lead time: None.
Damage   :   Virtually nil unless a structure becomes so contaminated by the poisonous substance that it requires destruction.
Casulties: Depending on the substance, could range from none to severe. Again, the elderly, particularly those with respiratory problems, will be more vulnerable than the general public.
Primary/ :   Rescue, evacuation, and warning. General
Long term   assistance and advocacy. Once more,
Action   it is likely that as with a NUCLEAR disaster, most poison disasters will see a quick and total federal involvement.

POLLUTION

This will be the sustained existence of polluting elements in the local atmosphere that, as it continues, makes breathing increasingly difficult and hazardous.

    Lead time: Self-generating.
    Damage : None.
    Casulties: Similar to those attending a HEAT WAVE.
    Primary/ : The same as for a HEAT WAVE.
    Long term
    Action.

TORNADO

A violent, twisting wind storm, generating winds of up to 300 mph at the center. Especially dangerous because of its unpredictable path.

    Lead time: A tornado watch may give up to several hours warning of the possibility but the actual appearance of a tornado generally gives little time to prepare.
    Damage : Nearly total in the path of the tornado, with the added problem that structures may be carried for miles.
    Casulties: Very great in path of storm.
    Primary/ : Because simple procedures can greatly
    Long term reduce casulties when there is a warning,
    Action tornado prone areas should stress these precautions. Otherwise, the agency should be prepared to assist in rescue operations and since victims are homeless, establish emergency food and shelter centers. Long term actions will include most normal advocacy programs.

Appendix·2

Interviewer's signature_____

CLIENT CASE RECORD

NAME_____AGE_____

PERMANENT ADDRESS_____PHONE_____

H O U S I N G :

Have you been re-located? YES____NO____.

If YES is it PERMANENT_____ or TEMPORARY?_____

ADDRESS_____PHONE_____

NAME OF HOST_____

Was your residence destroyed? YES____NO____

If not destroyed, what damage?_____
_____
_____

R E S I D E N T I A L   I N S U R A N C E :

Do you have insurance on your residence? YES____NO____

Does it cover your personal properties? YES____NO____

Have you contacted your insurance agent? YES____NO____

Has the Adjuster visited you? YES____NO____

Have you settled with the Adjuster? YES____NO____

Were you satisfied with the adjustment? YES____NO____

If NO, list reasons why:_____
_____

OTHER COMMENTS:_____

H E A L T H :

Do you have a disaster related injury or illness? YES___ NO___

    If YES, explain: _____

_____

Do you have a chronic medical condition? YES___ NO___

    If YES, is there immediate need for medication or treatment? YES___ NO___

_____

_____

Are there any disaster related losses of medical/health appliances (including glasses, false teeth, etc.)? YES___ NO___

_____

_____

T R A N S P O R T A T I O N :

Do you have an transportation? YES___ NO___

    If YES, provided by whom? _____

Was your car damaged by the disaster? YES___ NO___

    If YES, do you have adequate insurance? YES___ NO___

    Has your insurance agent or adjuster contacted you? YES___ NO___

    Were you satisfied with the adjustment? YES___ NO___

    If NO, list reasons why: _____

_____

C A S E   N A R R A T I V E :

Use page three (3) for case narrative and any additional comments.

Use this space for CASE NARRATIVE or other comments: _____

_____
_____
_____
_____
_____
_____
_____
_____
_____
_____
_____
_____
_____
_____
_____

Interviews at Disaster Assistance Center	Referrals made by Counselor
____ Food Stamps	NAME DATE
____ IRS	
____ Salvation Army	
____ Red Cross	
____ H.U.D.	
____ S.B.A.	
____ Legal Assistance	
____ Insurance	
____ Employment	
____ Un-employment	
____ Veterans	
____ Aging	
____ Individual and Family Grants	
____ Other: _____	
____ Other: _____	
____ Other: _____	

Appendix·3

LIST OF POSSIBLE LOSSES

LIVING AREAS
Floor coverings
Draperies, curtains
Sofas, couches
Upholstered chairs
Occasional chairs
Straight chairs
Pillows, slip covers
Tables
Desks
Secretaries
Planters, dividers
Floor lamps
Pictures, hangings
Mirrors
Clocks
Table lamps
Fireside fixtures
Accessories

BEDROOMS
Floor coverings
Draperies, curtains
Beds, springs
Mattresses
Dressers
Chests
Vanities
Chairs
Couches, benches
Tables, stand
Desks
Lamps
Pictures, hangings
Mirrors
Appointments
Cribs

YARD, GARDEN
Furniture, accessories
Cooking equipment
Mowers, sweep., trim.
Hose, sprinklers, tools
Garden implements

DINING AREA
Floor coverings
Draperies, curtains

KITCHEN, COOKING AREAS
Stoves
Refrigerators, freezers
Dishwasher, disposal
Rotisseries, roasters
Coffee makers, mixers
Toasters, waffle irons
Can openers, sharpeners
Cookware
Cutlery
Utensils
Liquors, wines
Foods
Clocks

UTILITY, APPLIANCES
Clothes washer, dryer
Mangles, irons
Sewing machines
Vacuum cleaners, polishers
Window air conditioners
De-humidifiers
Fans, heaters
Typewriters, add. mach.

ENTERTAINMENT
Piano, organ
Musical instruments
Television, radio sets
Hi-Fi, stereo
Tape, record players
Records, tapes

PERSONAL EFFECTS-Women's
Daytime dresses
Party dresses
Formals
Suits
Pant suits
Coats, jackets
Sweaters, skirts
Blouses
Slacks, jeans
Shorts
Beachwear
Sports wear
Hats, gloves, purses
Shoes, boots, slippers

PERSONAL EFFECTS-Men's
Suits
Sports coats, jackets
Slacks
Formal attire
Topcoats, overcoats
Shorts
Sweaters, raincoats
Shoes, slippers
Sport shirts
Dress Shirts
Beachwear
Belts, ties, socks
Hats, caps, gloves
Underwear
Handkerchiefs
Pajamas, robes
Jewelry, lighters

CHINA, CRYSTAL, LINENS
Dinnerware
China luncheon sets
Table cloths, linen sets
Napkins, mats
Goblets, glasses, tumblers
Punch bowls, pitchers

RECREATIONAL
Golf clubs
Fishing tackle
Guns, firearms
Tennis, bowling equipment
Cameras, projectors
Binoculars
Skates, ski equipment
Bicycles
Play equipment
Card tables, chairs
Toys, games, tools

BEDDING, BATH, MISC.
Blankets, spreads, quilts
Pillows, cases, sheets
Towels, wash cloths
Bath mats, curtains
Hair dryers
Electric razors, brushes
Electric blankets, sheets
Luggage

SILVER, SILVERWARE
Place settings
Serving, chafing dishes
Platters, trays
Dishes, bowls, pitchers
Tea and coffee services
Candle holders

PERSONAL PROPERTY WHICH USUALLY REQUIRES A SEPARATE INSURANCE POLICY
Jewelry, furs
Stamps, coins
Fine Arts

PERSONAL PROPERTY WHICH NEEDS SPECIAL ATTENTION
Autos, trucks
Boating equipment
Recreational vehicles

ANSWER SHEET

TEST NO. _____ PART _____ TITLE OF POSITION _____
(AS GIVEN IN EXAMINATION ANNOUNCEMENT - INCLUDE OPTION, IF ANY)

PLACE OF EXAMINATION _____ DATE _____
(CITY OR TOWN)   (STATE)

RATING

USE THE SPECIAL PENCIL.   MAKE GLOSSY BLACK MARKS.

Make only ONE mark for each answer. Additional and stray marks may be counted as mistakes. In making corrections, erase errors COMPLETELY.

ANSWER SHEET

SEP - - 2016

TEST NO. _____ PART _____ TITLE OF POSITION _____
(AS GIVEN IN EXAMINATION ANNOUNCEMENT - INCLUDE OPTION, IF ANY)

PLACE OF EXAMINATION _____ DATE _____
(CITY OR TOWN) (STATE)

RATING

USE THE SPECIAL PENCIL. MAKE GLOSSY BLACK MARKS.

Make only ONE mark for each answer. Additional and stray marks may be counted as mistakes. In making corrections, erase errors COMPLETELY.